THE ROLE OF
THE SUPREME COURT
IN AMERICAN GOVERNMENT

THE ROLE OF THE
SUPREME COURT IN
AMERICAN
GOVERNMENT

by

ARCHIBALD COX

OXFORD UNIVERSITY PRESS

London   Oxford   New York

OXFORD UNIVERSITY PRESS

Oxford   London   Glasgow
New York   Toronto   Melbourne   Wellington
Nairobi   Dar es Salaam   Cape Town
Kuala Lumpur   Singapore   Jakarta   Hong Kong   Tokyo
Delhi   Bombay   Calcutta   Madras   Karachi

printing, last digit: 10 9 8 7 6

PREFACE

THIS book consists essentially of the four Chichele Lectures delivered at Oxford University under the auspices of All Souls College early in 1975. I am grateful to All Souls for encouraging me to organize my thoughts, to Oxford for the lively and stimulating audience, and especially to John Sparrow, the Warden of All Souls, for his warm hospitality upon my visits.

The lectures were designed for a general university audience, all educated, some with sophisticated understanding of the U.S. Supreme Court but for the most part lacking professional legal training or specialized knowledge of American history and institutions. My purpose was partly expository—to show the kinds of questions with which the U.S. Supreme Court deals and the direction of recent decisions dealing with liberty and equality under a written constitution and Bill of Rights. The purpose was also partly jurisprudential—to face the currently pressing question, how far can and should the federal judiciary resolve by constitutional interpretation questions of public policy which are also fit for resolution through the political process? Both matters seem pertinent to British discussion of proposals for the adoption of a judicially enforceable Bill of Rights.

The lectures are presented here with only two kinds of revision.

First, freed from the constricting pressure of an undertaking to give four lectures of equal length, I found that the material in the third and fourth of the lectures logically belonged under three heads rather than two. The revision led me to expand the discussion of Equality and the Constitution and the Affirmative Duty of Government.

Second, I have added footnotes referring the reader to the cases discussed in the text and also to judicial decisions and other legal writing developing the points in more depth, in greater detail, or from a different point of view. The references are by no means exhaustive.

Because American scholars in constitutional law tend to focus upon specific topics, there are few general yet comprehensive works about American constitutional law. The reader who wishes to pursue the subject historically will find the most useful single volume to be Robert G. McCloskey, *The American Supreme Court* (1960). This admirable little book traces up to the 1950s the Court's chief contributions to the development of the American nation and the evolution of its constitutional law. Published in 1960, it could not deal with the momentous changes during the tenure of Chief Justice Warren, but it can be supplemented by Cox, *The Warren Court* (1967), or Bickel, *The Supreme Court and the Idea of Progress* (1970). More detailed histories are Charles Warren, *The Supreme Court in United States History* (2 vols., rev. ed., 1926); William F. Swindler, *Court and Constitution in the 20th Century* (2 vols., 1970).

Among the best sources of general commentary are *Selected Essays on Constitutional Law* (Ass'n. of American Law Schools, 1934–61); *The Supreme Court Review* (an annual collection of commentaries published by the University of Chicago Press); *Supreme Court and Supreme Law* (ed., E. Cahn 1954); A. Bickel, *The Least Dangerous Branch* (1962); C. L. Black, Jr., *The People and the Court* (1962); P. A. Freund, *The Supreme Court of the United States* (1961); Learned Hand, *The*

Bill of Rights (1958); Robert H. Jackson, *The Supreme Court in the American System of Government* (1955); H. Wechsler, *Principles, Politics and Fundamental Law.* Writings upon specific constitutional issues are cited in the footnotes at appropriate points.

Cambridge, Mass.   ARCHIBALD COX
July 1975

CONTENTS

INTRODUCTION

ALMOST a century and a half ago de Tocqueville observed, 'Scarcely any political question arises in the United States that is not resolved, sooner or later, into a judicial question.'[1] The statement is equally true today. Judge-made law plays a much larger part in the government of the American people than of the British. Our judges are less attentive to the letter of the law or to precedent. They move freely in wider orbits. Both bench and bar make greater use of statistical and other social studies, and the line between law and policy is often blurred. These characteristics reach their peak in constitutional adjudication by the Supreme Court of the United States and the inferior federal courts.

My aims in these lectures about constitutional adjudication are three:

The first is expository: even at the expense of ploughing well-tilled fields I seek to indicate the kinds of questions with which the Supreme Court deals and the extent of the constitutional protection accorded individuals and minorities.

The second purpose is to inquire into the uses and abuses of constitutional adjudication as an instrument of social policy. Here the emphasis will be less on results than on the proper institutional limits of the judicial function. The definition of these limits raises highly complex problems: with what kinds of public questions may the judiciary properly deal through the processes of constitutional adjudication? When may it deal with them? Given a justiciable constitutional controversy, how far should the court substitute its determinations for the

[1] De Tocqueville, *Democracy in America*, 1956, i. 280.

conclusions of Legislative and Executive? With respect to the construction of the language of the Constitution? With respect to the social or economic conditions said to support the measure challenged as unconstitutional? In balancing competing values? Again, given a justiciable constitutional controversy, how far is the court free to adopt what it believes the wisest public policy? How far is it bound by the constraints of precedent and other ingredients of law?

Third, the lectures inquire into the sources of the 'legitimacy' of the Supreme Court's constitutional decisions. Within the term 'legitimacy' I mean to include not only the notion of the Court's adherence to some charter, however vaguely defined, but also the ability to command acceptance, and compliance, which often means consent.

The second and third points are obviously interrelated. What the Justices should bring within the ill-defined boundaries that mark the limits of their charter depends partly upon their competency, that is upon whether the problem will yield to the judicial method, but also upon whether the political branches of government, the rest of the legal profession, and enough of the public will accept what the Justices do as legitimate and therefore as deserving of consent and support.

These three purposes underlie all five lectures. I hope that they have an interest of their own even for a British audience, but they are not irrelevant to the current discussion of whether the United Kingdom would benefit from abridging Parliamentary supremacy by adopting a written bill of rights which courts would enforce. For the U.S. Supreme Court decisions on the rights of individuals and minorities might presage the effects of such a safeguard; and consideration of the sources of the legitimacy of our constitutional decisions may throw a little light upon whether similar British institutions could command sufficient support.

I

THE SUPREME COURT
AND THE SYSTEM OF GOVERNMENT

I

EVEN the Watergate affair bears out de Tocqueville's observation upon the critical importance of law and courts in the American system of government. President Nixon's announcement that he would disobey a court order directing him to produce tapes and written memoranda covering nine Watergate conversations roused the public outburst which turned events towards impeachment. The decision of the U.S. Supreme Court ten months later sealed his fate, not merely by removing the last hope of legal justification for withholding more damning evidence, but psychologically by seeming to array the most respected branch of the government unanimously against him. The litigation over the Watergate Tapes, therefore, not only illustrates a major function of the federal judiciary but offers insight into the nature of our constitutionalism.

Two Watergate investigations were in progress in the spring of 1973. One, in the hands of a Special Prosecutor, was using a grand jury and other traditional processes of the criminal law. The second was conducted by a Select Committee of the U.S. Senate under the chairmanship of Senator Ervin with the aid of a large staff. Both were pursuing the two major lines of inquiry into white-collar conspiracies: (1) seeking to induce a conspirator near the top to give evidence against his associates; (2) obtaining documentary evidence. Documentary proof could be found only in White House files, and the White House would not make them available. John Dean told a story which, if true, made out a criminal conspiracy to obstruct justice on the part of the President, a former Attorney General, and key White House aides, but Mitchell, Erlichman, and Haldeman contradicted Dean. The whole matter seemed likely to turn upon their relative credibility unless corroborative documentary evidence were discovered. At the end of June 1973 the Special Prosecutor was about to initiate a test of his right of access to White House documents, including a taped recording or summary of one Presidential conversation which had come to his attention.

At this juncture another White House aide told Senate investigators that there were taped recordings of all conversations that had taken place in the President's offices. The news was given to an astonished country. The Special Prosecutor took out a subpoena *duces tecum* under seal of the district court, requiring production before the Grand Jury of the tapes and written memoranda recording nine specified conversations. The Senate Committee issued its own subpoena. Both were addressed to Richard M. Nixon as President of the United States, because the President had issued a statement that he alone had control of the tapes and files.

Recently, in private conversation, a Scandinavian legal scholar expressed his outrage at this course. 'It is unthinkable', he said, 'that the courts of any country should issue an order to its Chief of State.' My friend's indignation undoubtedly reflects an ancient postulate of many legal systems, including those that declared a monarch's abstract duty to obey the laws. About a century ago, the

Attorney General of the United States invoked this kind
of sovereign immunity in arguing in the Supreme Court
that the President is beyond the reach of legal process:

. . . I deny that there is a particle less dignity belonging to the
office of President than to the office of King of Great Britain or
of any other potentate on the face of the earth. He represents the
majesty of the law and of the people as fully and as essentially,
and with the same dignity, as does any absolute monarch or the
head of any independent government in the world.[1]

The Court dismissed the complaint, albeit upon somewhat
different grounds, but no suit against a president had
succeeded prior to the Nixon administration.

The claim of immunity could also be put—indeed it
was put—in terms more pleasing to American ears. The
Constitution is framed upon a theory of the separation
of powers. The federal legislative power is vested in
Congress, the executive power in a President elected
separately from the Congress, and the judicial power in
the courts. In theory, each of the three branches is
independent and co-ordinate with the others. A holding
that the President is personally subject to the orders of a
court—President Nixon's lawyers contended—would
effectively destroy the status of the Executive Branch as
an equal and co-ordinate element of government; *ex
hypothesi* one of three independent and co-ordinate branches
cannot dictate to another.

The two subpoenas could also be resisted upon grounds
of 'executive privilege.'[2] The Constitution says nothing
about executive privilege but a number of earlier Presidents,
including Dwight D. Eisenhower, had asserted that the
Chief Executive has the right to decide finally and for all

[1] *Mississippi* v. *Johnson*, 71 U.S. (4 Wall.) 475 (1866).
[2] The history of 'executive privilege' and judicial precedents are discussed in
Berger, *Executive Privilege* (1974); Cox, 'Executive Privilege', 122 U. of Pa. L.
Rev. 1383 (1974).

purposes what information, documents, or other papers in the Executive Branch of the government shall be kept confidential. The argument is partly in terms of the equality and independence of the three branches: no one branch, it is said, may control the documents or papers of another. The argument is also practical: in order to perform his constitutional duties the President needs aides and advisers with whom he can debate policy freely and candidly; and freedom and candour depend upon assurance of the confidentiality that protects a man from public or political reprisals because of what he has said or thought.

At this point two strategies were available to the President. He could refuse to participate in the judicial proceedings instituted by the Special Prosecutor to enforce the Grand Jury's subpoena, upon the ground that a President has a moral and constitutional duty to act upon his own interpretation of the Constitution in the performance of his Presidential duties. Or he could submit the same arguments to judicial determination. If the judgment went against him, he could still fall back upon the first alternative, although this would put him in the position of defying an adverse court decision instead of simply ignoring the courts. Still, the risk of losing might not seem large to one who agreed with my Scandinavian acquaintance that it is unthinkable that a mere judge would issue an order to the Chief of State.

President Nixon chose the latter course. Judge Sirica thought the unthinkable and ordered the President to produce the tapes and papers. The court of appeals affirmed Judge Sirica's order.[1] From there, an appeal lay to the Supreme Court.

At this point President Nixon switched signals. He would no longer submit the question to the courts. The

[1] *Nixon* v. *Sirica*, 487 F. 2d 700 (D.C. Cir. 1973), affirming 360 F. Supp. 1 (D.D.C. 1973).

nine tapes he would submit to Senator Stennis (a respected but exceedingly conservative Southerner sympathetic to executive power and secrecy) to decide what should be delivered, but the rest he would withhold, disregarding the judicial command. The other subpoenaed papers would be withheld, again disregarding the judicial command. As Special Prosecutor I was instructed to forgo future resort to the courts to obtain evidence withheld under claim of executive privilege. These steps were announced on a Friday night. I refused to obey the instructions, thinking to lay before the country the question of Presidential duty to obey the law as declared by the Judicial Branch. The next night the President dismissed me and terminated the independence of the Watergate Special Prosecution Force.

It is worth pausing to recall that courts have no power to enforce their decrees against the Executive. They possess neither the purse nor the sword. Constitutionalism as a constraint upon government depends, in the first instance, upon the habit of voluntary compliance and, in the last resort, upon a people's realization that their freedom depends upon observance of the rule of law. The realization must be strong enough for the community to rise up and overwhelm, morally and politically, any notable offender.

Nor can the people's response be taken for granted. In the beginning President Jefferson stood ready to defy the Supreme Court and he would have been successful, as I shall explain in a moment. Lincoln disregarded a habeas corpus at the start of the Civil War. Franklin D. Roosevelt was ready to take his case to the country if the Supreme Court invalidated one of his financial measures. During the debate over access to the first set of tapes I found myself deeply worried by the risk that President Nixon, who seemed to have an imperial view of the Presidency, might also be tempted to defy the courts. *His* Presidency had received an overwhelming popular endorsement less than a year before. The question of executive privilege might seem dryly technical. The people might think it unseemly for judges in lower courts to be issuing orders to the Chief of State. The evidence against the President was chiefly the testimony of John Dean and there were few, if any, signs that the country had turned against him. Suppose that the President's defiance were successful. The habit of compliance—the notion that a powerful executive official has no choice but to comply with a judicial decree—is a fragile bond. Who could say in an age of Presidential aggrandizement that if one President succeeded in his defiance, he and others might not follow that example until ours was no longer a government of law? How far was a man justified in provoking this kind of constitutional crisis with the outcome so uncertain?

My fears proved fantasies. President Nixon's announcement evoked a public reaction which his chief aide later described as a 'fire storm'. Within seventy-two hours the President changed his mind and promised to comply with the decree. A bit later, a new Special Prosecutor was appointed and the independence of the Watergate Special Prosecution Force was restored. The people proved their determination—and their moral and political power—to require the highest officials to meet their obligations under law.

I relate these events for three reasons:

First, they illustrate one of the principal functions of constitutional adjudication: the resolution of conflicts among different parts of our extraordinarily complex system of government, including disputes between the courts and the other branches.

Second, they raise the question: whence came the principle that even the President, the Chief of State, is subject to the rule of law, that is, to legal obligations under the Constitution and laws as declared by the courts?

You will not find the principle in the Constitution however carefully you read it.

Third, what are the sources and limits of the American people's attachment to constitutionalism—an attachment now so strong that it forced a popularly elected President to reverse his field and comply with the order of even an inferior court?

II

In a formal sense, the answers begin with the decision in *Marbury* v. *Madison* in 1803.[1]

The Presidential election of 1800 climaxed a political upheaval in which the Federalist Party yielded control of the Legislative and Executive Branches to the Jeffersonian Democrats. Thomas Jefferson supplanted John Adams as President of the United States. Most of the judges, however, were Federalists; and their tenure was for life. Just before leaving office President Adams and his Secretary of State executed the commission of one Marbury to be Justice of the Peace, but the Secretary forgot to deliver it. Ironically, the absent-minded Secretary was John Marshall, who was about to take office as Chief Justice of the United States and would write the opinion in the case resulting from his negligence. Secretary of State Madison, upon order of President Jefferson, withheld the commission. Marbury then brought an original suit in the Supreme Court seeking a writ of mandamus requiring Secretary Madison to deliver the commission.

President Jefferson and Secretary Madison were thus put to the same choice as President Nixon faced when the Special Prosecutor sought a judicial decree for the Watergate Tapes. Jefferson and Madison elected at the beginning simply to ignore the Court. Both were philosophically dedicated to asserting the independence, if

[1] 5 U.S. (1 Cranch) 137 (1803).

not the complete supremacy, of the elected representatives of the people. Both were politically committed to wresting the judiciary from Federalist control. In public debate their henchmen asserted a want of judicial power to issue orders to the Executive Branch.

The Court seemed to face Hobson's choice. To dismiss the case would apparently acquiesce in the Jeffersonian position. To issue the writ would invite President Jefferson and Secretary Madison to ignore it—a step they surely could and would have taken—while the country laughed at the Court's pretensions. Either result would confirm the independence of the Executive and Legislative from Judicial control.

The Court escaped the dilemma. Chief Justice Marshall first expounded the duty of the Executive to obey the laws and asserted the right of every citizen to judicial redress against executive illegality. He then determined that the refusal to deliver Marbury's commission was illegal, and also remediable by mandamus because the omitted act was ministerial. The stage seemed set for issuance of the writ, for an act of Congress gave the Supreme Court power to issue writs of mandamus in appropriate cases. But the Chief Justice took an unexpected turn. The act of Congress purported to give the Supreme Court original jurisdiction. The Chief Justice read the Constitution to say that in this situation the Court's only jurisdiction should be appellate. In such a case, he continued, it is the Court's duty to disregard the unconstitutional legislation; and this led to dismissal of the action. In this way the Chief Justice maintained the Federalist position of judicial supremacy over both the other branches of government upon questions of legal duty and constitutional interpretation, yet he avoided the issuance of a decree that President Jefferson would surely and successfully have disobeyed.[1]

[1] The best accounts of *Marbury* v. *Madison* and the struggle over the judiciary

As an act of judicial statecraft the opinion and decision in *Marbury* v. *Madison* were magnificent. The bold declaration that executive officials are subject to judicial correction when they violate a legal obligation provided the precedent necessary for subsequent rulings requiring even cabinet officers to refrain from unconstitutional invasions of private right and to perform their statutory duties. The most dramatic example prior to Watergate was a decree requiring the Secretary of Commerce to return to private owners the steel mills seized upon direction of President Truman in order to terminate a strike which had stopped essential production in time of war.[1] The Watergate case was novel because President Nixon's taking personal control over the tapes forced counsel to depart from the practice of naming only subordinates to the President as defendants, but to allow this substitution to govern the result would, as Judge Sirica observed, have exalted form over substance.

Marbury v. *Madison* also gave birth to the now familiar judicial power to rule upon the constitutionality of acts of Congress in the normal course of litigation. The decision made inevitable the establishment of a like national judicial authority over State legislation.[2]

So much is well known to those who have read American history. I repeat the familiar because of the dramatic contrast between the unenforcibility of the claims of the Judicial Branch in 1803 (if enforcement had been required) and the overwhelming moral and political support the identical claims received in 1973 when challenged by President Nixon. Something happened in the interval to give greater legitimacy to the constitutional judgments of the federal courts.

---

are Warren, *The Supreme Court in United States History*, ii. 169–316 (1926); Beveridge, *Life of John Marshall*, iii. 1–222 (1920).

[1] *Youngstown Sheet & Tube Co.* v. *Sawyer*, 343 U.S. 579 (1952).

[2] The existence of judicial power—indeed, judicial duty to give effect to the

III

Neither branch of the opinion in *Marbury* v. *Madison* finds such support in the words of the Constitution as would lead a citizen to say, 'This was ordained in the beginning'. Even a lawyer must strain to extrapolate supporting evidence from the words. Chief Justice Marshall's powerful opinion falls far short of conclusive demonstration.

To show that even the highest executive officials are subject to judicial control with respect to their legal obligations, the opinion simply assumes that citizens can have legal rights against officials acting in an official capacity, and then resorts to the assertion that if there were no judicial remedy, the government of the United States would cease to be 'a government of laws, and not of men'. The phrase is not in the Constitution. It is hardly self-evident that only judges can interpret the laws.

The opinion rests the power of the judiciary to rule upon the constitutionality of an act of Congress chiefly upon two arguments. The first invokes the judicial duty to find and apply the law in all cases coming on for normal adjudication:

if both the law and the Constitution apply to a particular case, so that the Court must either decide that case conformably to the law, disregarding the Constitution; or conformably to the Constitution, disregarding the law; the Court must determine which of these conflicting rules governs the case. This is of the very essence of judicial duty.[1]

Constitution rather than inconsistent State laws could not be denied in the face of Article VI quoted on p. 14 below. The hotly disputed question was whether the Supreme Court could review the decisions of State judges rejecting claims of federal constitutional right. The national power was sustained in *Martin* v. *Hunter's Lessee*, 14 U.S. (1 Wheat.) 304 (1816); *Cohens* v. *Virginia*, 19 U.S. (6 Wheat.) 264 (1821).

[1] 5 U.S. (1 Cranch) at 178.

The second argument asserts that the Court must give supremacy to the Constitution because that is the purpose of a written constitution:

The Constitution is either a superior paramount law, unchangeable by ordinary means, or it is on a level with ordinary legislative acts, and, like other acts, is alterable when the legislature shall please to alter it.[1]

If the former part of the alternative be true, then a legislative act contrary to the Constitution is not law: if the latter part be true, then written constitutions are absurd attempts, on the part of the people, to limit a power in its own nature illimitable.[2]

Between these alternatives, Marshall asserted, 'there is no middle ground'.[3] The force of the argument is self-evident, but it seems simplistic—which may have been a virtue—both in its absolutes and in its view of the process of constitutional adjudication.

It is quite wrong to say that there is no middle ground between concluding, on the one hand, that a legislative act which violates the Constitution is ineffectual or, on the other hand, that the Constitution, although written, is a nullity. Legislators may feel themselves bound by their own understanding of a written constitution even though the only sanctions are conscience and political pressure. The existence of an actual document also gives people a paramount standard by which to judge the conduct of their representatives. The irony in Chief Justice Marshall's argument is that the Supreme Court itself is limited in its interpretation of the Constitution only by its own self-restraint in responding to tradition, public pressure, and the claims of conscience in the performance of a judicial office. The real question, which Chief Justice Marshall never discussed, is whether a few judges appointed for life or the elected representatives of the people will better exercise the ultimate, uncontrollable

---

[1] Id. at 177.   [2] Id. at 177.   [3] Id. at 177.

power of determining what rules shall prevail in the areas arguably governed by the original charter.

Chief Justice Marshall's opinion is also subject to the criticism that it presents only the extreme case in which anyone can see whether the law is constitutional or not. Cases are not always so clear-cut, and in practice the close cases are typical. Throughout our history Supreme Court Justices have been rendering constitutional interpretations inconsistent with what other men of no less intelligence and integrity took to be the plain meaning of the words. The real question, again, is not the one which the Chief Justice presents; it is, whose view shall prevail upon a debatable point of interpretation: the view of the Court or of the President and the Congress. Indeed, the question is more complicated than this because the proper application of the Constitution in a given situation calls sometimes for the construction of the text, but usually for appraisal of disputed facts (including social and economic conditions), and for weighing the relative importance of opposing interests rather than construing words.

Chief Justice Marshall could have written a more sophisticated opinion, measured by current legal technique. Article VI of the Constitution provides: 'This Constitution and the laws of the United States which shall be made in pursuance thereof . . . shall be the supreme law of the land; and the judges in every State shall be bound thereby, anything in the Constitution or laws of any State to the contrary notwithstanding.'

Here it is ordained that State judges are to determine whether a State law conflicts with the federal Constitution, and to give precedence to the latter. They are also to give precedence to federal laws 'which shall be made in pursuance' of the Constitution. The latter phrase could mean 'duly enacted by the constitutionally ordained procedure', but it can equally well describe laws made by the federal government in the exercise of its constitutionally delegated power. The latter interpretation is consistent with the States' initial, strong desire to confine the power of the new federal government. If the latter interpretation be correct, then State judges were expected to inquire into the constitutionality of laws made by Congress, at least when they conflicted with State law; and if State judges were to exercise such power, it would hardly be denied the federal courts.

Extrinsic support can also be found for Chief Justice Marshall's ruling. The power of judicial review was asserted or assumed in half a dozen statements made during the Philadelphia convention. Similar statements were made to the ratifying conventions in the thirteen independent States. Number 17 of the Federalist Papers, written by James Madison, Alexander Hamilton, and John Jay in an effort to persuade the people of New York to ratify the proposed Constitution, ascribes the power to enforce constitutional limitations to the Judicial Branch. Other prominent public figures made similar statements between 1789, when the Constitution was adopted, and 1803, when *Marbury* v. *Madison* was decided. Indeed, one or two federal judges in the inferior courts had actually held acts of Congress unconstitutional, and State courts had held State legislation invalid because inconsistent with the State's fundamental law. The conclusion which the Court reached was also consistent with the colonists' experience under British constitutional law. The work of their legislatures had been subject to review for consistency with their charters, just as were the enactments of English municipal corporations.[1]

These bits and pieces, when cumulated, make a strong

---

[1] Scholars still debate whether Chief Justice Marshall's ruling conformed to the original understanding. The issue is extensively canvassed and the various points made here and elsewhere are documented in Berger, *Congress* v. *the Supreme Court*, pp. 8–285 (1969); Boudin, *Government by Judiciary*, (1932); Gunther and Dowling, *Constitutional Law—Cases and Materials*, pp. 15–23 (8th ed., 1970).

brief, but the argument hardly adds up to conclusive proof that the basic charter, as originally adopted, conferred supremacy upon constitutional questions to the Judicial Branch. Today, almost a century and three quarters later, the claims staked out in *Marbury* v. *Madison* have been validated by history: the system proved workable and the results, despite some egregious blunders, were generally acceptable. Of the forces shaping that history and the country's reaction, two seem to have been predominant: (1) the necessity for an umpire to resolve the conflicts engendered by our extraordinarily complex system of government; (2) a deep and continuing American belief in natural law. Of the two the first was surely the more important until thirty years ago.

IV

Again we must go back to the beginning. At the close of the American Revolution the thirteen former colonies became thirteen separate, sovereign, and independent States, each exercising all the domestic functions of a general government. The Constitution superimposed a new federal government with specifically delegated and limited powers. In the realm of foreign affairs and national defence the delegated powers are both exclusive and complete. In the domestic sphere they include almost unlimited authority to impose and collect taxes and to expend the sums collected for the general welfare. Other enumerated powers of great importance have proved to be the authority to borrow money on the credit of the United States; to coin money and regulate the value thereof; and 'to regulate commerce . . . among the several States'.

But the scope of the delegated powers is not clear from the words. To use a recent example, consider the Civil Rights Act 1964.[1] For decades in some of our

[1] Public Law 88–352, 78 Stat. 241, 42 U.S.C.A. ss 2000a *et seq.*

States, hotels, restaurants, lunch counters, and other places of public accommodation followed local custom in enforcing racial segregation and refused to serve black people if they had white patrons. Normally, it is for the States to inspect and regulate retail establishments. The rights of the businessman and his customers are usually governed by State law. A State would have indisputable power to require places of public accommodation to serve all would-be patrons to the limit of their capacity without regard to race or colour, but the States in which racial segregation was the custom would not enact such legislation. Could the federal government act? At first blush one might say, 'No'. There is no delegated power to regulate the service of food or race relations. The regulation of retail enterprises is a State function like protecting public health and safety and preserving public order. But suppose that the hotel caters to interstate travellers and the restaurant serves foodstuffs originating in other States. Could the federal government act under these circumstances upon the theory that it is exercising the granted power to regulate interstate commerce? What are the limits of the commerce power? How is the question to be resolved if Congress asserts the authority and a restaurant owner or a State denies it?[1] (Would not the United Kingdom be faced with a parallel question if exclusive authority to deal with some subjects were to be devolved upon Wales and Scotland and the Parliament in Westminster thereafter arguably legislated about one of the subjects delegated?)

A priori each branch of the federal establishment could be treated as the final arbiter of the scope of its own

---

[1] Such an assertion of federal power was sustained in *Katzenbach* v. *McClung*, 379 U.S. 294 (1964). A very useful review of the enormous expansion of federal power under the Commerce Clause following the critical 1938 decision in *National Labor Relations Board* v. *Jones & Laughlin Steel Corp.*, 301 U.S. 1, will be found in Stern, 'The Commerce Clause and the National Economy, 1933–1946', 59 Harv. L. Rev. 645, 883 (1946).

power. If the Congress decided that prohibiting racial discrimination in places of public accommodation would foster and promote the flow of interstate commerce and the President completed the legislative process by signing the enactment into law, that might be the end of the question. Under this view, self-restraint backed by conscience and popular political pressures would be the only sanctions enforcing the constitutional arrangement.

A second conceivable view, at the opposite extreme, is that each State, being a principal, has the power to call the federal government, its agent, to account for any act going beyond the scope of the agency power. This doctrine, once known as 'nullification' and later as 'interposition', would have given every State the right to veto any act of the federal government whose constitutionality it wished to question, subject only to any restraints of conscience upon what the State officials would call unconstitutional.[1] Had this doctrine prevailed, we could hardly have become one people bound in economic and political unity.

A third possible solution—the one chosen in *Marbury* v. *Madison* and confirmed by history—is to treat constitutional issues as questions of law to be decided by the courts *in the course of ordinary litigation*. Note the limitation. The courts do not decide abstract constitutional questions or render advisory opinions. The constitutionality of my hypothetical federal Equal Public Accommodations law would be tested after enactment whenever a restaurateur, sued by a black plaintiff for damages for a denial of equal

[1] The initial statements of the doctrine were by Thomas Jefferson and James Madison in the Kentucky and Virginia resolutions of 1800, Elliott, *Debates on the Federal Constitution*, iv. 540–80 (2nd ed., 1901). It was refined by theoreticians in the Southern States during the 1830s and 1840s, notably by John C. Calhoun. Bancroft, *Calhoun and the South Carolina Nullification Movement* (1928). Governor Faubus of Arkansas invoked the doctrine as late as 1958 in defence of his efforts to frustrate compliance with the school desegregation decisions of the U.S. Supreme Court. See *Cooper* v. *Aaron*, 358 U.S. 1 (1958).

accommodation or prosecuted in a federal court for the violation, chose to defend upon the ground that his conduct was not tortious or criminal because the federal statute, being beyond the constitutional power of the Congress to enact, was a nullity in court.

The federal system also produces a flow of converse questions concerning the validity of laws enacted by the States. The States retained a vast reservoir of sovereignty especially in relation to the public order, the ownership and transfer of property, commercial transactions, and nearly all the affairs of everyday life, but the Constitution imposed two sorts of restrictions. One sort is explicit; for example, the provisions forbidding the enforcement of any State law which is *ex post facto*, which constitutes a bill of attainder, or which impairs the obligation of contracts. Other restrictions, which are often only partial, may be inferred from the express grants of power to the federal government.

A good example was presented early in our history when the State of New York granted to one Livingston the sole right to operate steamships upon waters in the State of New York. Before the Constitution the grant would surely have been effective, but when the monopoly sued to enforce the law excluding other vessels, the defendants, whose vessels carried passengers from New York to other States, argued that the New York law was unconstitutional because the constitutional delegation of power to the federal government 'to regulate commerce . . . among the several States' should be understood as if the Constitution said that Congress and only Congress shall have power to regulate commerce among the States. A law enacted by Congress would prevail over any inconsistent State law;[1] but suppose that Congress had not acted. Was the State barred anyway? Was New York forbidden to enforce a monopoly against a steamboat

[1] The Supremacy Clause quoted at p. 14 above so provides.

carrying passengers or goods in interstate commerce in the absence of congressional action? Or did the Constitution leave a State free to apply its own laws to interstate commerce unless and until Congress exercised its power to regulate the matter? Common sense and the need for national unity dictated invalidation of the steamboat monopoly,[1] but it is not so easy to say that no State law may ever be applied to interstate transportation. Are steamships plying inland and coastal waters free to disregard the smoke control laws of the ports they enter?[2] The pilotage laws?[3] Should one conclude that the drivers of motor vehicles on interstate journeys need not observe local traffic regulations?[4] If the answer is that some State laws can apply to interstate commerce but others may not, what agency is to decide whether a particular State law falls in one category or the other?

The issue of State taxation raised similar questions. The States across which the great transcontinental railroads ran not unnaturally sought to levy tonnage taxes upon the freight carried. Was the tax permissible or implicitly forbidden by the grant to the federal government of power to regulate interstate commerce?[5] What about a tax upon gross receipts from interstate commerce?[6]

---

[1] *Gibbons* v. *Ogden*, 19 U.S. (9 Wheat.) 1 (1824), held the monopoly unconstitutional because inconsistent with federal licencing under an act of Congress.

[2] *Huron Portland Cement Co.* v. *City of Detroit*, 362 U.S. 440 (1960) (sustaining the enforcement of State law).

[3] *Cooley* v. *Board of Wardens*, 53 U.S. (12 How.) 299 (1851) (sustaining the enforcement of State law).

[4] Compare *South Carolina State Highway Dept.* v, *Barnwell Bros.*, 303 U.S. 177 (1938) (sustaining the application of the State law), with *Bibb* v. *Navaho Freight Lines, Inc.*, 359 U.S. 520 (1959) (invalidating the application of State Law).

[5] *Case of the State Freight Tax*, 82 U.S. (15 Wall.) 232 (1872) (holding the tax invalid).

[6] Although such a State tax was regarded as invalid for many years, there are intimations that such a tax may be valid if limited to gross receipts fairly apportionable to activity within the taxing State. Compare *Philadelphia & So. S.S. Co.* v. *Pennsylvania*, 122 U.S. 326 (1887), with *Central Greyhound Lines* v. *Mealey*, 334 U.S. 653 (1948).

On net income?[1]   On the local real estate?[2]   On the freight cars?[3]

Some method of deciding such questions was essential. To leave them to individual States to decide in the light of self-interest would have been incompatible with the need for a common market. It might have been left to Congress to decide whether each local regulation unduly burdened interstate commerce, allowing the local law to operate until Congress acted, but the size of the United States is so great that the willingness and ability of Congress to deal with all the multitude of little restrictions whose cumulative effect would none the less seriously clog interstate trade is open to question. As it happened, the Supreme Court asserted the right of the federal judiciary to decide such disputes as if they were matters of constitutional law. The Commerce Clause and the constitutional decisions under it made the United States a free trade area without sacrificing the benefits of a large measure of local self-determination.[4]

The peculiar nature of our federal system also gives rise to the need for some body to manage the interplay between State and federal law and State and federal

[1] Such a State tax is valid at least when the income taxed is fairly apportioned to activities within the taxing State. *U.S. Glue Co.* v. *Town of Oak Creek*, 247 U.S. 321 (1918).

[2] No one has ever seriously questioned the power of a State to tax local real estate even though used in interstate commerce.

[3] The rules concerning State taxation of the equipment of interstate carriers are complex and diverse. See, e.g., *Pullman's Palace Car Co.* v. *Pennsylvania*, 141 U.S. 18 (1891); *Standard Oil Co.* v. *Peck*, 342 U.S. 382 (1952); *Braniff Airways* v. *Nebraska Board*, 347 U.S. 590 (1954).

[4] State attempts to regulate and tax commerce illustrate some of the kinds of questions which some body must decide under a federal system and which did in fact fall to the federal courts, ultimately the U.S. Supreme Court. The body of constitutional law on both subjects is large and highly complex, especially with respect to State taxation of interstate commerce. The student interested in the rudiments will find helpful treatment in Frankfurter, *The Commerce Clause under Marshall, Taney and Waite* (1937); Sholley, 'Negative Aspects of the Commerce Clause', 3 U. of Chi. L. Rev. 556 (1936).

courts. Subject to the few express and implied restrictions, each State retains its sovereign power to govern. The federal government also has all the characteristics of a unitary government within its functionally limited sphere. The result is that within any territorial unit (any State) there are always two governments—State and federal—operating side by side but each sovereign and independent within its functional sphere. Each of us (unless an alien) has dual citizenship; he is a citizen of the United States and of the State in which he resides. Each pays two sets of taxes. Each may claim rights under two governments. Each is subject to two sets of laws, one State and one federal. Violations of a State law are subject to prosecution in the State court, violations of a federal law in a federal court. Civil cases may be brought in either the State or federal judicial system according to the nature of the cause of action.

But this is not all. The greatest complexities arise from the fact that the powers of the States and the federal government frequently overlap with respect to the subjects on which they are brought to bear, and both sets of courts —State and federal—apply both State and federal law, the State law being subordinated to the federal whenever there is conflict. Cases are appealed within the system in which they originate. In cases originating in the State courts the Supreme Court of the United States has appellate jurisdiction to rule upon a claim that federal law has not been correctly applied by the State court, but on all questions of State law the State court's decision is final. The presence of these two governments, two sets of laws and two sets of courts, both operating within the same geographical area and often upon the same persons and situations, but each sovereign within its own functional sphere, requires an umpire to keep the machinery working with some measure of harmony. Again, the function fell to the Supreme Court.

In 1920, long after the political unity of the United States was assured, Justice O. W. Holmes, Jr. observed: 'I do not think the United States would come to an end if we lost the power to declare an act of Congress void. I do think the Union would be imperiled if we could not make that declaration as to the laws of the several States.'[1]

Yet I wonder whether it was not essential to link the two powers, at least in the beginning. Although the Supreme Court and judicial review are instruments of federal control when examined from the viewpoint of the States, the power to inquire into the constitutionality of acts of Congress must have imparted some of the appearance and even of the reality of a truly neutral umpire standing outside the struggle. By good fortune the 'States' Rights' men who most resisted the Court's invalidation of State legislation were strict constructionists with respect to congressional power, and were thus disposed, at least some of the time, to hope for benefit from the Court's power to invalidate acts of Congress. Furthermore, the very existence of that alternative weakened the argument for a reserved State power to nullify what the State believed to be an unconstitutional act of Congress. It seems to me, therefore, that the assertion of judicial power to hold acts of Congress unconstitutional was also a building-block of national unity, accepted as necessary to make the system work.

v

The problem of the Watergate Tapes illustrates another quite different sort of problem in the division of governmental power. Where lies the final authority to determine what information or documents in the Executive Branch shall be kept secret when a court, on the one hand, or the Congress, on the other hand, requires the informa-

[1] O. W. Holmes, Jr., *Collected Legal Papers* (1920), pp. 295–6.

tion? The question is different because it arises out of the separation of powers within the federal government rather than between the Nation and the States.

Even within the federal government the distribution of power is extraordinarily complex. As I remarked earlier, the Constitutional Convention, distrusting strong government and profoundly influenced by Locke and Montesquieu, divided the federal government into three equal and co-ordinate branches, each often said to be independent of the others. In truth, each is given considerable power to check the others. Congress may enact laws, but the President may veto bills passed by Congress (although Congress by sufficient majorities may override the veto). When a bill becomes law, the manner of its administration depends upon the Executive Branch—a discretion of enormous importance in an age in which legislation must be written in general terms. The President may appoint men to aid him in executing the laws, but his appointments are subject to confirmation by the Senate, and a strong Congress can use its power to withhold appropriations as a lever.

The separation of powers produces many conflicts among the three branches, especially between the Legislative and the Executive. Some controversies can be shaped as disputes over whether a branch has asserted power not granted to it by the Constitution, but to another, so that its purported action is a legal nullity. What is the effect of the President's purporting to dismiss an employee of the Executive Branch despite an act of Congress requiring Senate approval?[1] Will an executive agreement made as a phase of the President's recognition of a foreign government supersede State law governing the title to property formerly belonging to

---

[1] Compare *Myers* v. *United States*, 272 U.S. 52 (1926) (upholding dismissal of postmaster) with *Humphrey's Executor* v. *United States*, 295 U.S. 602 (1935) (holding dismissal of a member of Federal Trade Commission invalid).

foreign nationals, without ratification by the Senate ?[1] Has the Chief Executive, in the absence of legislation, authority to take control over industrial property in order to terminate a potentially disastrous labour dispute in time of war ?[2] May a President use the armed forces in combat outside the United States ?[3] At first blush one is tempted to leap to the conclusion that the Supreme Court, as the authoritative voice of the Constitution, could and should resolve such disputes in the same manner as between the Nation and the States; and indeed the Court has ruled upon many such questions in situations in which a private person suffered legal injury as a result of the contested action. Thus, the Court decided that the Constitution gives the President exclusive power to dismiss officials he appoints because the power is executive, but that he may not, without statutory authority, seize private industrial property to terminate a labour dispute even in time of war because the decision whether to deal with critical labour disputes in such a fashion, under the Constitution, is for Congress, the Legislative Branch.

VI

Not all disputes between the President and Congress are resolvable by the Supreme Court even when they raise constitutional issues. Many of our constitutional questions are non-justiciable, as in Britain. There were two subpoenas for the Watergate Tapes: one issued on behalf of the Grand Jury, the second by the Senate Watergate Com-

[1] *United States* v. *Pink*, 315 U.S. 203 (1935) gave an affirmative answer.
[2] See note 1, p. 11 above.
[3] The above question became a matter of fierce controversy during American military involvement in Indo-China in the 1960s and 1970s. Among the convenient sources are Senate Report No. 797, 90th Cong., 1st Sess. (1967); Note, 'Congress, the President, and the Power to Commit Forces to Combat', 81 Harv. L. Rev. 1771 (1968); Symposium, 'Legality of United States Participation in Viet Nam Conflict', 75 Yale L.J. 1084 (1966).

mittee. In answer to both the President pleaded the executive privilege said to be impliedly granted by the Constitution. The issue was promptly adjudicated in the first case. The Senate Committee encountered such obstacles as to discourage the House Judiciary Committee from seeking a judicial determination when it tried to subpoena additional tapes in the proceedings tending towards impeachment.

The difference is explained by the fundamental theory of judicial review. The Judicial Branch is charged with adjudicating legal 'cases' or 'controversies'—in plain words, with deciding ordinary lawsuits involving the actual or threatened invasion of the kind of legal right the courts are accustomed to recognize. The power to rule upon constitutional questions is an incident of this duty. As Chief Justice Marshall put it in the beginning: 'if both the law and the constitution apply to a particular case, so that the court must either decide that case conformably to the law, disregarding the constitution; or conformably to the constitution, disregarding the law; the court must determine which of these conflicting rules governs the case.'[1]

The courts ruled upon the claim of executive privilege as a defence to the subpoenas obtained by the Special Prosecutor because it arose in the course of normal judicial business: a grand jury inquiry into possible crimes in the one case,[2] and the trial of a criminal indictment in the other.[3] But resolving disputes between the President and Congress over the provision of evidence for the Congress is not part of, or incident to, any judicial business confided to the courts by the statutes that presently define their jurisdiction;[4] and therefore the

[1] *Marbury* v. *Madison*, 5 U.S. (1 Cranch) 137, 178 (1803).

[2] *Nixon* v. *Sirica*, 487 F. 2d 700 (D.C. Cir. 1973), affirming 360 F. Supp. 1 (D.D.C 1973).

[3] *United States* v. *Nixon*, 418 U.S., 683 (1974).

[4] The jurisdiction of the federal courts is wholly statutory. When the Ervin

courts cannot now rule upon the effect of congressional subpoenas. For generations such quarrels over claims of executive privilege *vis-à-vis* Congress were everywhere regarded as typical examples of constitutional issues not subject to adjudication; they came to be called 'political questions'.

Recently a bill was introduced in the United States Senate to establish a law office under congressional control which would be empowered to test claims of executive privilege and other alleged executive usurpations of the powers belonging to Congress, including, I presume, such matters as the use of the armed forces outside the United States without a congressional declaration of war.[1] The proposal illustrates the trend of which I spoke in the beginning—the tendency to take more and more of the political business of government to the courts for adjudication as justiciable questions of constitutional interpretation. The question arises whether the strains upon the judicial process would not become excessive in terms not only of judicial competence but of the judicial as opposed to the political quality of the resulting decisions.

The Court is not without its defences if it chooses to invoke them. The Constitution confines the federal judicial power to 'cases' and 'controversies'.[2] These are words of

---

Committee brought an action for judicial enforcement of its subpoena for sundry Watergate Tapes, the U.S. District Court dismissed the complaint for want of the necessary statute conferring jurisdiction. *Senate Select Committee* v. *Nixon*, 366 F. Supp. 51 (D.D.C. 1973). A special law was enacted conferring jurisdiction to enforce subpoenas of the Ervin Committee but a new action was dismissed by the District Court because the ensuing publicity might prejudice the anticipated criminal trials and this judgment was affirmed upon the ground that the Ervin Committee had failed to show that the information was 'demonstrably critical to the responsible fulfillment of the Committee's functions'. *Senate Select Committee* v. *Nixon*, 370 F. Supp. 521 (D.D.C. 1974), affirmed, 498 F. 2d 725, 731 (D.C. Cir. 1974).

[1] See p. 25, note 3.
[2] Article III.

art long held to bar the Court from accepting other, non-judicial business. Although the proposed legislation would provide a statutory basis for jurisdiction to rule upon claims of executive privilege *vis-à-vis* Congress, there are two grounds upon which the statute might be held unconstitutional. First, it is arguable that no judicially cognizable 'case' or 'controversy' arises where the dispute is confined to two political branches of the government and does not directly affect any individual's liberty or any private material interest. Second, there is a rule that the courts will not intervene unless there are judicially manageable standards for resolving the constitutional issues.[1] The inability of the courts to articulate any precise or acceptable rules delimiting Presidential authority to use the armed forces outside the United States, or to acquire the information and make the evaluations necessary to apply any verbal formulas they might articulate, best explains the courts' refusal to rule upon the constitutionality of the President's use of the armed forces in Indo-China.[2] The same difficulty could be pressed against efforts to empower the Judicial Branch to rule upon a President's claims of executive privilege in relation to the Congress without including some legislative definition of the precise scope of his duty. Behind these doctrines requiring 'standing' and 'judicially manageable standards' lies the policy of avoiding weakening the courts by embroiling them *unnecessarily* in the turbulent waters of political controversy.

But 'unnecessarily' is a term of degree. The tendency in recent years has been to liberalize the test of 'case' or

---

[1] The above themes are more fully developed in the works cited on p. 5, note 2, above.

[2] e.g., *Mora* v. *McNamara*, 389 U.S. 934 (1967); *Homes* v. *United States*, 391 U.S. 936 (1968); *Massachusetts* v. *Laird*, 400 U.S. 886 (1970). The suggestion in the text above is elaborated in Cox, 'The Role of Congress in Constitutional Determinations', 40 U. of Cincinnati L. Rev. 199, 201–6 (1971). Compare Varel, 'The War in Viet Nam', 16 Kan. L. Rev. 449 (1968).

'controversy' and so expand the judicial function. The political scientist sees the Court as the organ chiefly responsible for the structure of government. The constitutional scholar concentrating upon the judicial function gives a similar description. Interpreting the Constitution is the bulk of the Court's work, and this is what the layman observes. It is hardly surprising, therefore, that less emphasis is now placed than it was forty years ago upon confining the performance of these functions to conventional law suits. Nor is it certain that the expansion of the Court's role is wrong. The counsel of caution was ardently advocated when the Court was asked to treat the malapportionment of representatives in Congress and the State legislatures as a justiciable, constitutional violation. The Court overrode the objections, entered the political thicket, and emerged stronger than before.[1] For the present, therefore, let me leave the question open until my final lecture, as only one of many instances of the wider role the Court is under pressure to perform.

VII

In conclusion, it may be helpful to summarize in a positive fashion what I have been trying to say in the preceding pages. The doctrine of judicial supremacy and the people's attachment to this form of constitutionalism drew their principal sustenance from the rich soil of necessity. Without a supreme expositor upon the constitutional distribution of power and popular acceptance of its decisions, the enterprise upon which the American people launched

[1] *Baker* v. *Carr*, c69 U.S. 186 (1962); *Reynolds* v. *Sims*, 377 U.S. 533 (1964). These decisions holding that disputes over the apportionment of seats in a legislative body are justiciable and that the Equal Protection Clause requires equal representation *per capita* are the subject of vast commentary. A useful article is McKay, 'Reapportionment: Success Story of the Warren Court', 67 Mich. L. Rev. 223 (1968). For an excellent, full study see Dixon, *Democratic Representation in Law and Politics* (1968).

themselves in the Constitution could hardly have survived. With the Court as expositor the system worked so well that history legitimated the power, and then habit took over to guide men's actions so long as the system worked well enough. I do not mean to minimize the Court's role as the guardian of human rights or the strength which the doctrine of judicial supremacy drew from American acceptance of natural law. Yet I wonder whether the latter alone would have been enough, and the doubt may raise a question as to how far one could safely draw upon the American experience for evidence about the feasibility of transporting constitutional adjudication to the British environment as an adjunct only to a Bill of Rights.

II

THE COURT AND INDIVIDUAL LIBERTY

We all know that this Assembly . . . have no power to restrain the Acts of succeeding Assemblies . . . and . . . therefore to declare the Act to be irrevocable would be of no effect in law . . . [But] we are free to declare, and do declare, that the rights asserted are of the natural rights of mankind, and that if any Act hereafter be passed to repeal the present . . . such Act will be an infringement of our natural rights.—*Virginia Act of 1786 for Establishing Religious Freedom.*

I

BELIEF in natural rights and natural law were deeply ingrained in the eighteenth-century American mind despite uncertainty whether their source was the King of Kings and Lord of all the earth, the immutable maxims of reason and justice, or the accumulated wisdom of English common law. The conviction that there were such natural rights made it easy to express them in a Constitution, and then to accept the notion that a duly enacted statute in conflict with natural rights was not a binding law. In the debate upon proposals which were to become the first ten amendments to the United States Constitution, known as the Bill of Rights, James Madison predicted: 'independent tribunals of justice will consider themselves in a peculiar manner the guardians of those rights; they will be an impenetrable bulwark against every assumption of power in the Legislative or Executive.'[1] Others were willing to go still further. When Supreme Court Justice William Johnson, a Jeffersonian, could find no provision in the Constitution denying a State power to revoke its own prior land grants, he none the less ruled: 'I do not hesitate to declare that a State does not possess the power of revoking its own grants. But I do it on a general principle, on the reason and nature of things: a principle which will impose laws even on the Deity.'[2]

This early belief in the supremacy of natural law and its survival into our own time, albeit with different intellectual trappings and under other names, helped to secure acceptance of the legitimacy of judicial supremacy on matters of constitutional interpretation.

Alongside the commitment to natural law there developed an equally profound but logically inconsistent conviction that the people are the source of all legitimate power, that governments are the people's agents, and that the people, expressing themselves through the majority, have the right to work their will. The ambivalence gave rise to lasting problems in defining the proper role of the Supreme Court in dealing with questions of individual liberty. The legislatures, State and federal, represent the theme of popular sovereignty. The Supreme Court, when enforcing constitutional restrictions in the interest of the individual, is the voice of natural law. Given judicial supremacy in matters of constitutional interpretation, it is also for the Court to judge between the Legislative Branch and itself, to determine how and where to strike the balance between the two opposing themes. The questions are of judicial method and the analysis becomes complex but at bottom the answers determine

---

[1] Annals of Congress 439 (1789).
[2] *Fletcher* v. *Peck*, 10 U.S. (6 Cranch) 87, 143 (1810) (concurring opinion).

how much of the business of government shall be reserved to the people and the political process and how much should go to the judges, ultimately to the Supreme Court of the United States, under the label 'constitutional law'.

For a little more than three-quarters of a century after the U.S. Civil War the conflict between the two themes was focused in litigation challenging national and State minimum wage, maximum hours, labour relations, workmen's compensation laws, rate regulation, and similar legislation required for an urban, industrialized society. Many such laws were nullified as unconstitutional under the Fifth and Fourteenth Amendments, which forbid the federal government or any State to 'deprive any person of life, liberty or property without due process of law'. The courts read into this sweeping declaration such natural rights as liberty of contract, enjoyment of the fruits of property, and pursuit of a natural occupation. The judges would then examine the alleged justification for the statute, appraise its value and, balancing this against the individual right, render their usually adverse-to-the-statute decision. In *Adair* v. *United States*[1] the Court held that Congress could not constitutionally prohibit a railroad from discharging workers who joined a labour union because the prohibition interfered with liberty of contract. *Lochner* v. *New York*[2] invalidated a State law restricting employment in a bakery to ten hours a day; the Court judged the health hazards of longer hours insufficient to justify the sacrifice of liberty of contract. The volume of nay-saying rulings reached its peak during the mid-1930s in the face of rising political demand for State and national action to halt the Great Depression and adjust the imbalance created by corporate and financial power.

Most of us now agree that such decisions were badly wrong; the question is, where did the Justices get off the

[1] 208 U.S. 161 (1908).   [2] 198 U.S. 45 (1905).

track? Was the mistake simply due to a failure to understand the nature and needs of modern industrial society? Or was it also institutional because the Court had taken over parts of the business of government which belong to the Legislative Branch, not to the Judiciary? To be specific, why should a court give constitutional protection to a 'liberty of contract' which the Constitution does not mention? Why should nine men appointed for life have the final word in appraising the dangers of long hours of work in a bakery and weighing them against the invasion of liberty after a legislature has already performed that very function? The era was marked by vigorous reaction against natural law and a strong movement towards legal relativism and positivism. Historians and political scientists were 'proving' that judicial review was a usurpation of power defeating the original intent. There was a sense that the Justices made a mess of things when they attempted to enlarge their orbit, as they did in resisting government regulation of the economy. There was fear that the Court must destroy confidence in its decisions and lose the ability to command voluntary acceptance if it persisted in defying the popular mandate expressed by the political branches.

In 1937, in the face of President Roosevelt's court-packing plan, the Justices retreated.[1] Soon there were changes in personnel. A philosophy of judicial deference to legislative determinations rapidly became dominant among the Justices and the lower-court judges, and also in the law schools and legal profession. The rule became that the courts should never—or hardly ever—read specific rights such as 'liberty of contract' into the Due Process Clause. Nor should they balance such rights against the interests served by the challenged legislation

---

[1] The turning point is marked by *National Labor Relations Board* v. *Jones & Laughlin Steel Corp.*, 301 U.S. 1 (1937) and *West Coast Hotel Co.* v. *Parrish*, 300 U.S. 379 (1937).

unless, perhaps, the legislation was patently arbitrary and capricious. 'We have returned to the original proposition that courts do not substitute their social and economic beliefs for the judgment of legislative bodies, who are elected to pass laws.'[1]

In the 1930s a modest view of the judicial function in constitutional interpretation fitted the new generation's desire for progressive social and economic reform. The legislative and executive branches were engaged in the redistribution of power and the protection of the disadvantaged and distressed. By the 1950s the political atmosphere had changed. The legislative process, even at its best, became resistant to libertarian, humanitarian, and egalitarian impulse. At worst, the legislatures became repressive, in the libertarian view, because of the Cold War, increased crime, the fear of social disorder, and, perhaps, the strength of established economic and political power.

I do not mean to imply that the spirit of reform was dead. Egalitarianism was strengthened by the rise of the peoples of Asia and Africa, both in their native lands and in the places to which they had been transported. The multiplication and magnification of government activities intensified fears for individual liberty. Later, a wave of subjectivism bred wide dissatisfaction with all constraints. But in the new era these impulses were not shared so strongly and widely as to realize themselves through legislation. They came to be felt after the early 1950s by a majority of the Supreme Court Justices, perhaps by the fate which puts one man upon the Court rather than another, perhaps because the impulses were felt more strongly in the world of the highly educated.

The result was a revival of the activist judicial

---

[1] *Ferguson* v. *Skrupa*, 372 U.S. 726, 730 (1963). See also *Olsen* v. *Nebraska*, 313 U.S. 236 (1941); *Lincoln Federal Labor Union* v. *Northwestern Iron & Metal Co.*, 335 U.S. 525 (1949); *Williamson* v. *Lee Optical Co.*, 348 U.S. 483 (1955).

philosophy, first in relation to free speech, the press, and political liberty, then in the area of race relations, but rapidly spreading to other spheres. The ultimate protection for minorities, for spiritual and political liberty, for freedom of expression, and other personal liberties— it was said—comes rightfully from the judiciary. In these realms the political process, subject to arbitrary compromises and responsive as in some degree it must be to short-term pressures, is inadequate to enforce the long-range, enduring values that bespeak our better judgment. A majority of the Court under Chief Justice Warren came to be influenced by an extremely self-conscious sense of judicial responsibility for minorities, for the oppressed, for the open and egalitarian operation of the political system, and for a variety of 'rights' not adequately represented in the political process.

At the same time the losers in the political process were becoming more conscious of the potentials of constitutional adjudication for achieving goals not attainable through political weapons. More and more litigation came to be conducted by civil rights and civil liberties organizations, by radical political associations, and later by law offices funded to stimulate community action and provide legal services to the poor. Each successful appeal to the courts in lieu of the political process added to the momentum from previous steps. More and more of the problems of government were being presented to and handled by the federal courts as questions of constitutional law. There was rapid reinterpretation of the Constitution.

I have chosen three issues to exemplify the changes in the nature of constitutional adjudication: freedom of expression, the right of privacy, and the promotion of equality under the Fourteenth Amendment.[1]

---

[1] The debate within the Court over the proper scope of the judicial function in constitutional cases is exemplified by the several opinions in *Board of Education*

II

Freedom of inquiry, and of thought and debate, we in the academic world know to be the best hope of progress towards the truth we can never know for certain. Suppression of speech is also an affront to the human personality because a man burdened with an idea has a need to express it. 'Speech concerning public affairs is more than self-expression; it is the essence of self-government.'[1]

The extent of the constitutionally protected freedom of the press to publish information it acquires concerning the conduct of government is exemplified by the case of the Pentagon Papers.[2] Daniel Ellsberg made copies of highly secret, classified papers involving military operations and diplomatic negotiations which had been entrusted to him in confidence. He abstracted the copies and gave them to newspapers for publication. The Executive asked the courts to enjoin publication, making strong representations that the risks of injury to national interests included 'the death of soldiers, the destruction of alliances, the greatly increased difficulty of negotiation with our enemies, the inability of our diplomats to negotiate . . . and the prolongation of the war'.[3] The Court ruled that such risks would not support an injunction against publication, even for the period necessary to study how far the fears were justified.

---

v. *Barnette*, 319 U.S. 624 (1943); *Adamson* v. *California*, 332 U.S. 46 (1947); *Barenblatt* v. *United States*, 360 U.S. 109 (1959); *Griswold* v. *Connecticut*, 381 U.S. 479 (1965).

The professional commentary is voluminous. See, e.g., Bickel, *The Supreme Court and the Idea of Progress* (1970); Black, *The People and the Court: Judicial Review in a Democracy* (1960); Brown, 'The Supreme Court, 1957 Term Forward', 72 Harv. L. Rev. 77 (1958); Cox, *The Warren Court* (1968); Hand, *The Bill of Rights* (1958); Rostow, 'The Democratic Character of Judicial Review', 66 Harv. L. Rev. 193 (1952); Wright, 'Professor Bickel, the Scholarly Tradition and the Supreme Court,' 84 Harv. L. Rev. 769 (1971).

[1] *Garrison* v. *Louisiana*, 379 U.S. 64, 74-5 (1964).
[2] *New York Times Co.* v. *United States*, 403 U.S. 713 (1971).
[3] Id. at 762.

The Pentagon Papers decision does not guarantee the press absolute freedom. There were three dissenters. Four Justices in the majority declined to embrace the absolutism of Justices Black and Douglas, who declared that *ever* to permit *any* prior restraint upon publications of *any* news would 'make a shambles of the First Amendment'.[1] (One wonders whether they would have ruled during World War II that a newspaper had a constitutional right to publish for Nazi eyes the knowledge that, because of the work at Bletchley, British authorities were reading the orders of the Nazi High Command.) Two Justices in the majority suggested the possibility that publishing government documents 'leaked' in breach of security regulations might constitutionally be punished as a criminal offence. These interesting and potentially important questions were left open, and they ought not to obscure the main point. All the weight of the Executive was insufficient to bar disclosure of highly secret and sensitive documents concerning the conduct of pressing military and diplomatic affairs.

The expansion of the freedom of the press is most dramatically exemplified by changes in the law of libel and of contempt of court. Throughout most of Anglo-American history both public and private persons have been awarded damages for the injury done by the publication of a false and defamatory statement of fact. In 1960 the *New York Times* published an advertisement, purchased by civil rights leaders, which an Alabama judge and jury found to contain false and defamatory statements about the conduct of a police commissioner during a civil rights demonstration. He was awarded $500,000 for actual and punitive damages. The Supreme Court reversed, overruling 175 years of settled legal practice, and held that the First and Fourteenth Amendments bar a State from awarding a public official damages for a

[1] Id. at 715.

defamatory falsehood relating to his official conduct unless the falsehood is published with knowledge of its falsity or with reckless disregard for whether it be true or false.[1] The rule denies recompense to the victim of libel even upon proof that the reporter or publisher failed to exercise due care. Conversely, it assures the newspaper reporters, editors, and publishers that they need not worry about having to pay damages to public officials whom they injure by carelessly publishing false and defamatory statements of fact.

Later cases extended the immunity to libels upon senior civil servants, candidates for office, football coaches at State universities, and sundry other public figures, such as a physicist and a retired army general who had issued statements upon public issues.[2]

For a time it seemed probable that the Court would extend this immunity to all news reports and commentaries, even about persons previously unknown to the public,[3] but in the summer of 1973 a splintered Court pulled back.[4] Robert Gertz was a Chicago lawyer who had represented the family of a man killed by a Chicago policeman under circumstances causing public controversy. Gertz had belonged to leftist organizations and played very minor roles in community affairs. Robert Welch, Inc., an organ of the John Birch Society, published an article purporting to expose a left-wing conspiracy against the police which contained false and defamatory statements about Gertz. When Gertz brought an action for libel, the publisher set up the *New York Times* defence.

The Supreme Court held that Gertz was not a public

[1] *New York Times Co.* v. *Sullivan*, 376 U.S. 254 (1964).

[2] *Rosenblatt* v. *Baer*, 383 U.S. 75 (1966) (manager of municipal recreation facility); *Curtis Pub. Co.* v. *Butts*, 388 U.S. 130 (1967) (football coach); *Associated Press* v. *Walker*, 388 U.S. 130 (1967) (retired army officer).

[3] *Rosenbloom* v. *Metromedia, Inc.*, 403 U.S. 29 (1971).

[4] *Gertz* v. *Welch, Inc.*, 418 U.S. 323 (1974).

figure because he 'had achieved no general fame or notoriety in the community' and did not 'thrust himself into the vortex' of the particular public controversy. The Court then pronounced three rules:

(1) The Constitution gives absolute freedom to publish statements about public figures which turn out to be false and defamatory unless the publisher knew them to be false or was reckless as to their truth.

(2) The Constitution frees the press from liability where there is neither negligence nor more serious fault.

(3) Injury must be proved; it cannot be presumed from the bare publication of a libel, and the damages may not exceed 'actual injury' unless the falsehood was intentional or reckless.[1]

The *Gertz* case was decided by the Burger Court. The earlier Warren Court might have extended the *New York Times* rule to all publications. The libertarian enthusiasm may have cooled, but the freedom from risk of liability which the Burger Court has accepted is more significant than what little is left of the law of libel. The American press is now in a greatly improved position to pursue investigations into corruption and other abuses of public position. It seems likely that much of the early reporting upon Watergate and related scandals would not have been attempted under the older law. Similarly, a visitor to England gets the rough, though unconfirmed, impression that the danger of libel suits inhibits the British much more than the American press, and that this affects the democratic process.

The American press has also been freed from the fear of prosecution for contempt of court because of commentary upon pending judicial business, however strident the effort to arouse public pressure to influence the course of justice. In *Wood* v. *Georgia*[2] the judge, who had charged a grand jury to investigate the sale of Negro votes in a

---

[1] Id. at 348–50.   [2] 370 U.S. 375 (1962).

local election, was accused of racial bias, hypocrisy, and
political intimidation and persecution in a public letter
to the grand jury demanding that it drop the investigation.
The letter was held to be protected by the First Amendment. The decision would equally license the dominant
newspaper in a rural county in the deep South to try to
stop a grand jury inquiry into suppression of Negro
voting by attacking as a subversive, radical hypocrite the
judge who initiated the investigation.

Similarly, the press has been freed to publish gory
accounts of crime and sensational evidence against the
accused prior to trial, even though the consequences
must be delay of the trial, change of venue, or possibly
dismissal of the indictment upon the ground that an
untainted jury cannot be assembled.[1]

On one side, this rule seems a sorry sacrifice of sobriety
and decency in the administration of justice; and I am
afraid that too many American attorneys use the skills of
advertising and public relations men to influence public
opinion on behalf of their clients instead of trying cases
before judge and jury exclusively upon the evidence.
Yet the Watergate affair illustrates the value of the rule
at least in the case of charges against high public officials.
The wide publicity served the extraordinary purpose of
enabling a whole people to sit in judgment upon its highest
political leaders, to pass judgment upon whether they
were fit to be leaders, to deliberate upon the proper
standards of public responsibility, and not merely to
decide whether they were guilty or innocent of crime.
The value of that exercise in self-government—and I am
convinced of its authenticity—seems to me to have out-
weighed any risk of unfairness at the trial of these former
leaders (assuming, of course, that the jurors sincerely
believed that they could decide upon the evidence adduced
in the courtroom). The case seems different when the

---

[1] *Maryland* v. *Baltimore Radio Show*, 338 U.S. 912 (1950).

crime nowise affects the conduct of public business, but it is difficult to perceive just how and where to draw a line. In the latter cases, moreover, the danger that newspaper publicity arousing public passion will result in unjust convictions—as distinguished from unjust acquittals—is reduced by rules of court and departmental regulations restricting pre-trial statements or the release of evidence by prosecuting attorneys, the police, or others who may be regarded as officers of court.[1]

I do not mean to imply that the press has invariably had its way. In *Branzburg* v. *Hayes*[2] a newspaper reporter refused to answer questions for a grand jury concerning illegal drug traffic he had personally observed, claiming that the First and Fourteenth Amendments give a reporter freedom not to disclose his sources of information, and to decide how much he will disclose of what he has learned. The argument, pressed by a thunderous chorus of editors and reporters, was that if a reporter is forced to reveal in court or before a grand jury information given in confidence, then particular sources of such information will dry up, all to the diminution of the free flow of information protected by the First Amendment. Reporters had never had this privilege. A bare majority of the Supreme Court adhered to the existing law and put the needs of the administration of justice first. The question remains highly controversial, but for the present it is enough to say that a press secure from interference in a zone extending out from the core of liberty as far as the close balance of judicial opinion upon this question indicates, has little to fear in the way of interference or suppression.

Earlier I quoted the dictum: 'Speech concerning public

---

[1] A useful study of the entire problem of publicity affecting criminal trials is 'American Bar Assn. Project on Minimum Standards for Criminal Justice, Standards Relating to Fair Trial and Free Press' (1966).

[2] 408 U.S. 665 (1972).

affairs is more than self-expression; it is the essence of self-government.'[1] Self-government, as the Warren Court perceived it, begins with lusty and uninhibited debate over issues, candidates for office, and the conduct of officials and other public figures. The decisions build upon an inherited tradition, but the vision from which they spring encompasses greater turbulence and faster changes in society than the intellectual liberalism of the eighteenth and nineteenth centuries. There must be room not only for false accusations but for coarse expletives and affronts to personal and public sensitivities, and for far-out, radical political movements; care must also be taken not to interfere with their use of the streets and unorthodox methods of expression. Far-out groups so extreme as to frighten or annoy all 'right-minded' people have little access to the conventional channels of effective expression. For them the best vehicles of expression are sit-ins, picketing, marches, and mass demonstrations. Their language like their tactics is often aimed to shock the community.

Even without empirical studies it is safe to surmise that the chief danger to freedom of expression by the poor, the unorthodox, and the unpopular, lies in licensing ordinances and other general laws that vest wide discretion in local authorities to maintain the peace and public order. In recent years the Supreme Court has proved remarkably sensitive to the danger that such laws will be abused. One doctrine, traceable to the 1930s, is that a law requiring a licence for the use of the streets or parks for demonstrations, parades, or other forms of expression must explicitly confine the licensing authorities to considerations of traffic control, crowd control, and interference with other ways of preventing inconvenience or menace to the public. Broader discretion, it is said, not only creates excessive risk of discrimination but may

[1] *Garrison* v. *Louisiana*, 379 U.S. 64, 74–5 (1964).

induce an applicant to mince words that are constitutionally protected, in order to get or keep a licence.[1] From
there it is only a short step to holding that a man may
not be punished for words or for a street demonstration
under a broad, general rubric, such as breach of the peace,
which leaves wide discretion to the police, public prosecu-
tors, and judges, and thus invites discrimination based
upon distaste for the views expressed rather than a fair
judgment upon the risk of violence.[2]

A related doctrine holds that the Court will reverse the
conviction of a speaker or demonstrator without regard
to whether his conduct could be punished constitutionally
under a different statute, if the statute under which he
was convicted was drafted so broadly that the authorities
could apply it unconstitutionally to someone else. For
example, in *Gooding* v. *Wilson*[3] it appeared that anti-war
pickets had blocked access to an Army building in
violation of a police request. During the scuffle which
ensued when the police sought to clear the way for Army
recruits, a picket said to a policeman, 'White son of a
bitch, I'll kill you', and again, 'You son of a bitch, I'll
choke you to death.' The picket was convicted under a
statute punishing as a misdemeanour the 'use to or of
another and in his presence . . . [of] opprobrious words
or abusive language, tending to cause a breach of the
peace'. The Supreme Court purported not to decide
whether the speaker had a constitutional right to say
what he did, but set aside the conviction, by a 7–2 vote,
upon the ground that the statute was 'susceptible of
application to protected expression'. In another case the
defendant, in a public meeting of the school board attended
by women and children had, as the law report states,
'used the adjective, "M— F—", on four occasions to

---

[1] e.g. *Lovell* v. *City of Griffin*, 303 U.S. 444 (1938); *Cantwell* v. *Connecticut*, 310 U.S. 296 (1940).

[2] *Cantwell* v. *Connecticut*, 310 U.S. 296 (1940). [3] 405 U.S. 518 (1972).

describe the teachers, the school board, the town, and his own country'. The defendant was convicted under a statute prohibiting 'indecent' and 'offensive' language in public places. This conviction also was reversed upon the ground that in another case the statute might be applied to constitutionally protected expression.[1]

The ostensible theory of the doctrine is that an over-broad statute is itself a threat to freedom of speech which the Supreme Court removes by a declaration of unconstitutionality. Of course the declaration does not take the statute off the books, and it is also the rule that it can be rendered valid and enforceable by a narrowing interpretation by the highest State court. At this point one wonders whether the entire doctrine is not built upon pretence. How many people likely to be involved in this class of cases read the statutes and ordinances closely enough to be deterred from constitutionally protected speech by an over-broad law, and then follow the law reports with such care as to be reassured by a Supreme Court decision declaring the law unconstitutional on its face unless and until it is saved by a narrowing construction by the State's highest tribunal? And how many check for narrowing State court interpretations? Nor has the Court given any sign that it has faced the problems of the draughtsmen and has some notion of how to write a law which covers the endless variety of conduct that may disturb public order or decency yet cannot be twisted to reach some constitutionally protected form of expression.

I refer to these vulgarities partly to show how the doctrine of over-breadth can be run into the ground but also partly to raise another question: Does the guaranty of freedom of speech leave any scope for legislation designed to protect the moral, aesthetic, or patriotic sensibilities of the community, or to preserve the tone of

[1] *Rosenfeld* v. *New Jersey*, 408 U.S. 901 (1972).

public discourse? One suspects that most of the Justices
voting to reverse the convictions in the offensive language
cases upon the ground of over-breadth were really ready
to hold that there is no room for such State action under
the First and Fourteenth Amendments.

The problem is illustrated by *Cohen* v. *California*.[1]
Cohen, a young man opposed to both conscription for
military service and the war in Vietnam, expressed his
protest by walking about in public places wearing a shirt
with the boldly printed, coarse and vulgar slogan, 'FUCK
THE DRAFT'. He was arrested and convicted for 'maliciously
and wilfully disturbing the peace ... by offensive conduct'.
The Supreme Court reversed the conviction in an opinion
written by the late Justice Harlan, the most gentle and
gentlemanly of Justices and a man of impeccable taste and
sensitivity. Justice Harlan gave three reasons for concluding that the 'First and Fourteenth Amendments must be
taken to disable the States from punishing public utterance
of this unseemly expletive in order to maintain what they
regard as a suitable level of discourse within the body
politic.'[2]

First, verbal tumult, discord, and offensive utterances
are in truth only the necessary side-effects of removing
governmental restraints from public discussion in order
that the decision as to what ideas and emotions shall be
voiced, and how they shall be voiced, shall be put in the
hands of each of us individually, in the faith that experience in the use of such freedom to choose will ultimately
produce a more capable citizenry and more perfect polity.
No other approach would comport with the premise of
individual dignity and choice upon which our political
system rests.

Second, the State can at best strike only at the most
extremely offensive words, yet it can offer no principled

[1] 403 U.S. 15 (1971).   [2] Id. at 23.

distinction between words it must tolerate and those it would forbid.

Third, citizens unsophisticated in the use of language often choose coarse vulgarities to convey otherwise inexpressible emotions, and the communication of emotions is as important a part of public discourse as the explication of intellectual ideas. The vulgarities uttered at the school board meeting mentioned earlier are examples of this point, for the expressions are the language of black protest aimed at shocking and thus jarring the white middle class out of its inbred assumptions. Perhaps no other words would have quite served the purpose.

There is force to the arguments; perhaps they should carry the day, but they leave me less than convinced. Surely the State has power to regulate the decorum of judicial proceedings, and I would suppose that the power includes the preservation of dignity by barring words spoken to be offensive though not relevant to the issues. The State may do this because dignity is conducive to reasoned justice and also builds respect. Why should the rule be different at public hearings held by a school board? There is no less interest in preserving the tone of the proceeding; there is also an interest in general attendance and great likelihood of driving away those who would rather abstain than subject themselves to sheer vulgarity. What then about public discourse? Is there no State interest in the level at which public discourse is conducted? Granting that the State can do little to protect moral and aesthetic sensibilities or to raise the level of public discourse, does it follow that the State must allow exhibitionists and other persons trading upon our lower prurient instincts to inflict themselves upon the public consciousness and dull its sensibilities? One wonders, too, whether the Supreme Court in extending the protection of the First Amendment to sheer vulgarity, useful only in its ability to shock, does not give the

vulgarities an imprimatur which contributes to the lowering of public discourse. The moral influence of the Supreme
Court's opinions reaches far beyond the limits of its
decrees[1]. May not its amoral influence be similarly
extended?

The issue of obscene publications raises similar
questions when related to the First Amendment. Here
again the law has been revolutionized. The current
areas of debate involve only the outermost fringe of a
vastly expanded area of freedom of expression. The
decisions of the 1960s seemed to be moving towards the
view that the State has no power to punish the sale,
exhibition, or other commercial distribution of porno-
graphy to consenting adults,[1] but recently the Court, by a
5–4 vote, held that the States and federal government
may punish as a criminal offence the commercial exhibition or distribution of a picture or writing which 'depicts
or describes in a patently offensive way sexual conduct
specifically defined by the applicable ... law', provided that
'the work taken as a whole lacks serious literary, artistic,
political, or scientific value'.[2] The test is apparently to be
whether the material is explicitly and specifically focused
upon pictures or descriptions of ultimate sexual acts or
of the genitals. The Chief Justice declared that a State
does have an interest 'in the quality of life and the total
community environment' and in 'the tone of commerce
in the great city centers'. 'The sum of experience including
that of the past two decades, affords an ample basis for
legislatures to conclude that a sensitive key relationship
of human existence, central to family life, community
welfare, and the development of the human personality
can be debased and distorted by crass commercial
exploitation of sex.'[3]

[1] *Stanley* v. *Georgia*, 394 U.S. 557 (1969).
[2] *Miller* v. *California*, 413 U.S. 15 (1973)
[3] *Paris Adult Theatre* v. *Slaton*, 413 U.S. 49, 63 (1973).

Taken as a whole, the free speech decisions of the past twenty years have expanded liberty and strengthened self-government. The few I question are, at worst, minor blemishes. The gains make it especially interesting to contrast the Warren Court's conception of its proper scope and function with the conception held by its much criticized predecessors which supported economic *laissez-faire*.

First, the free speech cases make it plain that the Court is once again finding facts and balancing opposing values in the manner so much criticized when the old Court was dealing with economic regulation. The validity of the reporters' claim of a First Amendment privilege not to disclose sources of information was decided on the results of two inquiries: (1) just how justified *in fact* were the fears of the press that sources of information would dry up if the courts continued to treat reporters like other citizens as regards information needed in the administration of justice; (2) if some sources of information dried up, would the losses outweigh the gains of the testimony. In the *Gertz* libel case Justice Powell's opinion for the five-member majority followed the technique of a common-law jurist balancing opposing interests without precedent to control him. On the one side, Justice Powell took the interests to be the circulation of information and debate upon matters of public significance; on the other, the individual's right to dignity and worth. In the case of a public figure, the Court held, the imposition of liability for anything less than an intentional or reckless falsehood carries too much risk of self-censorship resulting in suppression of truth; but the scales are tipped in favour of a private person because a private person, unlike a public figure, does not voluntarily expose himself to risk of falsehood, and lacks opportunity to command attention to his reply. Plainly, the decisions reached reflect the Justices' view of wise policy rather than anything to be found in the Constitution.

Second, some of the decisions, notably the libel cases, take the responsibility for large areas of law away from the States, centralize it in Washington, and thus reduce the opportunities for growth through experimentation.

In a third respect, the Warren Court behaved even more like a Council of Wise Men and less like a court than the *laissez-faire* Justices. The decisions of the 1950s and 1960s forced changes in the established legal order. *New York Times Co.* v. *Sullivan* overturned the law of libel as it had prevailed from the beginning. One could easily multiply examples. A nay-saying court engaged in invalidating novel legislation upon constitutional grounds seldom needs to overrule previous decisions. A reforming court must constantly overrule precedent, change established practices, and thus undermine the belief that judges are not unrestrainedly asserting their individual or collective wills, but following a law which binds them as well as the litigants.

A fourth notable characteristic of the Warren Court leads in the opposite direction. Whereas the *laissez-faire* decisions of the first third of the present century overturned legislation with strong popular support and frustrated the interests of masses of people, the free speech decisions, viewed realistically, seldom ran counter to any express will of the people and affected them only indirectly. For example, the law of libel was made by judges; the over-broad statutes and ordinances found unconstitutional scarcely expressed a conscious popular will concerning particular borderline applications.

To apply the philosophy of judicial self-restraint to the area of speech and press would entrust those liberties to the substantially uncontrolled power of the individual States and the Congress. In the historical context the very presence of the Bill of Rights in the Constitution implies that its framers intended to provide restrictions upon legislative power over certain areas of human activity in which liberty was deemed especially important. To the question of why the Court should distinguish between freedom of expression, on the one hand, and economic liberty and property, on the other hand, the answer can be given that the Constitution is relatively more specific in the guarantees of the First Amendment.[1] If specific mention in the Bill of Rights is itself not a charter for especially active judicial intervention, such mention can at least serve as a workable demarcation line separating those areas in which the Court must play an active role, because activism is necessary to get good results, from other fields in which the Court is likely to do more harm than good and thus should defer to the will of the people.

But can the line be so drawn? And will it? If it is not drawn here, where can and should it be drawn? Or should no line be attempted?

The 1973 abortion cases dramatically show the Court in the process of resolving just such questions.

III

In each of the abortion cases[2] a pregnant young woman was reluctant to bear the child for some personal reason involving no serious danger to life or health. In each case she lived in a State in which it would be a crime for a doctor to perform the abortion, either under a nineteenth-century law making it a crime to 'procure an abortion' except 'for the purpose of saving the life of the mother', or under a modern statute liberalizing the grounds for abortion but still not as permissive as the particular case would require. In each instance the young woman asked a court to enjoin the State authorities from prosecuting any doctor who might abort her, upon the ground that the

---

[1] The suggestion runs through many of the opinions assigning a 'preferred position' to the 'specific guarantees of the Bill of Rights'. See p. 36, note 1 above.

[2] *Roe* v. *Wade*, 410 U.S. 113 (1973); *Doe* v. *Bolton*, 410 U.S. 179 (1973).

threat of prosecution under the statute interfered with her exercising a form of personal liberty secured by the Fourteenth Amendment guarantee against deprivation without due process of law.

How should such a case be decided? Justice Frankfurter, Judge Learned Hand, and the other apostles of judicial self-restraint would have no trouble upholding the constitutionality of the statutes. At most, they would have said, the courts may do no more under the Due Process Clause than invalidate a law that no one could rationally believe to be related to some public interest; and no one could sensibly claim that an anti-abortion law fails this test. Justice Black would have reached the same conclusion. He had dissented in an earlier case holding that a married couple has a constitutional right to use contraceptives, saying:

I do not believe that we are granted power by the Due Process Clause or any other constitutional provision or provisions to measure constitutionality by our belief that legislation is arbitrary, capricious or unreasonable, or accomplishes no justifiable purpose, or is offensive to our own notions of 'civilized standards of conduct' . . . The use by federal courts of such a formula or doctrine or whatnot to veto federal or state laws simply takes away from Congress and States the power to make laws based upon their own judgment of fairness and wisdom and transfers that power to this Court for ultimate determination . . .[1]

The Supreme Court, by a 7–2 vote, nevertheless held the anti-abortion laws unconstitutional. The Constitution, the Court said, guarantees 'certain areas or zones of privacy'. Having an abortion because of personal preference is an aspect of privacy. Since privacy is a 'fundamental right', any State interference must be justified by some 'compelling interest'. That interest, the opinion continues, cannot be in the 'life' of the foetus because no one can say except by arbitrary definition when 'life' begins; nor

[1] *Griswold* v. *Connecticut*, 381 U.S. 479, 513 (1965).

can it be the interest in 'potential life' prior to the seventh month of pregnancy, for until then the foetus has no capacity for independent existence. The necessary compelling interest cannot be found in the health of the mother during the first six months of pregnancy, because medical statistics show that the dangers to health are greater in childbirth than in abortion; but the State may regulate abortion procedures during the third three months in the interests of health because of the statistically higher risks to health in that period. Oddly, but possibly because counsel did not stress the point, the opinion fails even to consider what I would suppose to be the most compelling interest of the State in prohibiting abortion: the interest in maintaining that respect for the paramount sanctity of human life which has always been at the centre of western civilization, not merely by guarding 'life' itself, however defined, but by safeguarding the penumbra, whether at the beginning, through some overwhelming disability of mind or body, or at death.

Finding the medical case against abortion unpersuasive, the Court laid down three rules:

(1) During the first three months of pregnancy the State must leave the decision whether to have an abortion, and when and how to carry it out, to the woman and her doctor.

(2) During the second three months the State may not forbid abortion but may regulate the procedure.

(3) The State may prohibit abortion after six months except when necessary to preserve the life or health of the mother.

For one concerned with the proper role of the Supreme Court in American government and more particularly with the debate over judicial activism the abortion cases have three-fold significance:

First, the decisions plainly continue the activist, reforming trend of the Warren Court. They are 'reforming' in the sense that they sweep away established law supported by the moral themes dominant in American life for more than a century in favour of what the Court takes to be the wiser view of a question under active public debate.

Second, the Justices read into the generalities of the Due Process Clause of the Fourteenth Amendment a new 'fundamental right' not remotely suggested by the words. Because they found the right to be 'fundamental', the Justices felt no duty to defer to the value judgments of the people's elected representatives, current as well as past. They applied the strict standard of review applicable to repression of political liberties.

Third, three Justices in the seven-man majority were appointed by President Nixon as 'strict constructionists': Chief Justice Burger, Justice Blackmun who wrote the opinion of the Court, and Justice Powell. Only one Nixon appointee dissented. There are ample signs that the Burger Court will not respond to new libertarian and egalitarian values with all the enthusiasm of its predecessor, and also that it is more worried by some of the complexities, cross-currents, and needs for accommodation that refuse to yield to optimistic generalizations. A court more concerned with the preservation of old substantive values than with articulation of a new spirit will find fewer occasions for rendering activist decisions. Still, the abortion cases strongly suggest that the new Justices are not restrained by a modest conception of the judicial function but will be activists when a statute offends their policy preferences.

In the end, therefore, one comes to the question: has the Court swung around the circle back to the method which led to equating Due Process with the economics of *laissez-faire*. Is there any *general* principle which authorizes the Court to substitute its judgment for the result of the political process when dealing with abortion but not

with hours of work? To read liberty of abortion into the
Fourteenth Amendment but not liberty of contract? If
not, which judicial method was right and which wrong?
Before one proposes to judge by results and not by method,
one has also to ask how a purely eclectic, result-oriented
approach would affect the Court's standing and utility.[1]

[1] See p. 112.

III

EQUALITY AND THE CONSTITUTION

THE constitutional litigation of any era reflects the aspirations and divisions of the contemporary society. No other force operating in the second half of the twentieth century approaches in importance the pressures generated by the coming of age of the peoples of Asia and Africa. In the United States the issue was—and is—between better realization of the promise of the Declaration of Independence, that all men are created equal, and adherence to ways of life rooted in the habits of people, North as well as South, since before the signing of the Declaration.

Despite its professed ideals, U.S. society long relegated the black man to a largely separate and always inferior social, economic, and political position. In the southern States, segregation of blacks as an inferior caste was commanded by law as well as custom. In other States, the law and political theory were more nearly even-handed, but in practice there was widespread racial discrimination. The old rules of constitutional law, including the accepted distribution of governmental power between States and Nation, did little to facilitate and much to obstruct the correction of these racial injustices by force of law. The pressure for racial equality built up during the 1940s and 1950s put the Supreme Court of the United States at the centre of a social and political revolution seeking accomplishment within the frame of constitutionalism if possible, yet ready if necessary to burst the bonds of law.

I

The initial response was *Brown* v. *Board of Education*.[1] The Fourteenth Amendment commands: 'nor shall any State deny any person within its jurisdiction the equal protection of the laws'. This constitutional mandate, the Court said, is violated by any State or local school district created by a State which segregates children in different schools according to race or colour. Later cases extended the holding to other racial segregation laws.[2] The *Brown* decision restated the spirit of America and provided a beacon of hope for black men at a time when other governmental voices had nothing to offer.

The result can only be described as a revolution in constitutional law. State laws enforcing a caste system which segregated black from white from birth through burial were invalidated, and enforcement gradually stopped. The command of the Fourteenth Amendment is addressed only to government: 'nor shall any State deny . . . the equal protection of the laws'; but new doctrines were developed extending this constitutional prohibition against racial discrimination to private decisions in activities specially encouraged or supported by a State.[3] New federal statutes were enacted in order to deal with acts and practices depriving black citizens of the right to vote, and to secure for them equal treatment in places of public accommodation, equal employment

[1] 347 U.S. 483 (1954).

[2] e.g. *Mayor and City Council of Baltimore* v. *Dawson*, 350 U.S. 877 (1955) (municipal beaches); *Holmes* v. *City of Atlanta*, 350 U.S. 879 (1955) (golf courses); *Johnson* v. *Virginia*, 373 U.S. 61 (1963) (seating in courtroom).

[3] e.g. *Shelley* v. *Kraemer*, 334 U.S. 1 (1948); *Burton* v. *Wilmington Parking Authority*, 365 U.S. 715 (1961); *Reitman* v. *Mulkey*, 387 U.S. 369 (1967). But see *Evans* v. *Abney*, 396 U.S. 435 (1970); *Moose Lodge* v. *Irvis*, 407 U.S. 162 (1973).

opportunities, and equal access to housing.[1] Constitutional law changed and grew in order to sustain the new federal laws. Propelled by the decision, the courts later struck down a multitude of legal discriminations based upon sex, alienage, length of residence, illegitimacy of birth, and sometimes (but less often than one would wish) ability to pay.[2] The egalitarian influence of *Brown* also ran strong in the decisions reforming the administration of criminal law by requiring the States to supply paupers, in both courts and police stations, with the legal assistance that others can buy.[3]

To enact a statute or hand down a judicial decision does not automatically change the way men live. Racial discrimination and disadvantage are still all too common. The forward movement has slowed partly because of the 'Southern strategy' of the Republican Party and partly, I suspect, because rapid social reform uses up social energy. But it is also clear that accomplishment is everywhere, and that the face of America has permanently changed.

The civil rights revolution and related egalitarian pressures raised a variety of intensely difficult problems of constitutional adjudication. One group involves the formulation and enforcement of remedies for previous unconstitutional discrimination in the public education, in other words school desegregation—an issue to be discussed later as one instance of the use of constitutional adjudication to impose affirmative obligations upon government rather than merely to block governmental oppression.[4] Another group illustrates the difficulty in giving meaning to the phrase 'equal protection of the law'.

---

[1] Civil Rights Act of 1964, 78 Stat. 241; Voting Rights Act of 1975, 79 Stat. 437; Civil Rights Act of 1968, 82 Stat. 73.

[2] See pp. 69–75 below.

[3] e.g., *Griffin* v. *Illinois*, 380 U.S. 609 (1965); *Miranda* v. *Arizona*, 384 U.S. 346 (1966).

[4] See pp. 76–90 below.

The problems parallel those discussed in the previous lecture concerning the Due Process Clause.

II

The constitutional requirement of '*equal* protection of the laws' cannot possibly mean that a State must treat everyone exactly alike. Classification is an inescapable part of government. The Fourteenth Amendment does not require a State to allow an almost blind man to drive an automobile because it grants licences to those with perfect vision. A State may regulate the sanitary conditions in a restaurant even though it does not regulate garages. It may allow optometrists to grind eye-glasses but forbid opticians to do so. It may grant financial aid to the blind and withhold it from the deaf. On the other hand, the Equal Protection Clause obviously forbids some kinds of classification. A State may not deny persons of Oriental descent the opportunity to pursue an occupation open to Anglo-Saxons or debar them from the inheritance of real estate. The Court's problem under the Equal Protection Clause is to articulate some general principle or principles by which to separate constitutional from unconstitutional differentiations.

Note that this is not simply a matter of deciding which classifications are good, or just, or desiderable. Also involved is the question of how much discretion in setting up a classification of debatable wisdom should be left to the States, partly for local rather than national determination and partly as fit for the political processes which determine the will of the people.

During the era of popular sovereignty and judicial self-restraint described in my second lecture three rules were established:

(1) A classification is constitutionally permissible which has *some* reasonable basis in terms of *some* rational view of the public interest.

(2) If a set of facts could conceivably exist that would render a classification reasonable, their existence must be assumed.

(3) Since evils in the same general field may be of different dimensions and proportions—or so a legislature may think—legislation may be addressed to one phase neglecting the others.[1]

To illustrate, a State agency with power to train and license Mississippi River pilots was held not to have violated the Equal Protection Clause by preferring the sons and nephews of pilots for apprenticeship because instilling a tradition linked to familial interest could be supposed to be the best way of providing safe and effective pilotage.[2] Similarly, a law was upheld which forbade the operators of trucks to lease space on the sides for advertising other business but which allowed the operators to advertise their own businesses.[3]

III

Then came the problem of racial segregation. The opinion in *Brown* v. *Board of Education* condemned racial segregation in the schools because it 'deprives children of minorities of equal educational opportunities'.[4] Plainly, the Court was not applying customary constitutional principles. Better academic achievement is surely a 'reasonable' goal of educational policy. Honest men not only could, but many do, conclude after serious study that the academic progress of children is greater when the races are segregated. To meet such arguments, the Supreme Court, bearing in mind 'the historical fact that the central purpose of the Fourteenth Amendment was to eliminate

[1] *Lindsley* v. *Natural Carbonic Gas Co.*, 220 U.S. 61 (1911); *Williamson* v. *Lee Optical Co.*, 348 U.S. 483 (1955). The classic discussion is Tussman and tenBroek, 'The Equal Protection of the Laws', 37 Cal. L. Rev. 341 (1949).

[2] *Kotch* v. *Board of River Port Pilot Commissioners*, 330 U.S. 552 (1947).

[3] *Railway Express Agency* v. *New York*, 336 U.S. 106 (1949).

[4] 347 U.S. at 493.

racial discrimination emanating from official sources in the States', created the special rule that 'racial classifications' are 'constitutionally suspect', 'subject to the most rigid scrutiny', and 'in most circumstances irrelevant to any constitutionally acceptable legislative purpose'.[1]

At first glance the notion that racial classifications, being invidious, require extraordinary justification, seems simple and desirable enough, but complexity soon develops. Suppose that a vacancy occurs in a racially mixed, public housing project. Ten families apply, one white and nine black. There should be equality of opportunity without regard to race, you will say; selection should be according to need, or priority of application, or some other racially neutral principle. Suppose further that experience shows that if the percentage of black families in a public housing project exceeds an established figure, the white families will leave the project, ending the racial integration. Racially integrated housing is widely believed to be a desirable measure, perhaps one of the best ways to overcome prejudice and resulting discrimination against minorities. Suppose that our hypothetical housing project is just at the tipping-point. Must the State award the vacancy to the black family entitled by colour-blind rule or may it discriminate against that particular family because it is black and prefer the white family because it is white, in order to benefit the black minority generally by residential integration? When we speak of 'equality of opportunity' whose, and what, opportunity are we to focus upon? The particular black family's opportunity to get this housing? The opportunity to live in a racially mixed community? The opportunities of black people generally to overcome the obstacles resulting from slavery and segregation?[2]

Consider another variant. In America State universities

---

[1] *McLaughlin* v. *Florida*, 379 U.S. 184, 192 (1964).
[2] For further discussion of 'benign quotas', see Bittker, 'The Case of the Checker

are bound by the Equal Protection Clause. A few years ago the Law School of the University of Washington had 1601 applications for an entering class to which 275 men and women could be admitted with the expectation that enough would actually enroll to fill 150 places. An applicant was given the option to disclose that he or she belonged to one of four minority groups: Black, Mexican-American, American-Indian, or Filipino. Every applicant was assigned an index number designed to predict his first-year grades in law school by extrapolation from his score on a Law School Aptitude Test (LSAT), combined with his grades during his last two years in college. There is widespread belief that, given the difficulty of making truly individual judgments upon personal characteristics, selection of the applicants with the highest predicted first-year averages, either with or without adjustments to take into account other evidence of more promising academic performance, results in the admission of the students with the greatest intellectual promise in law school work insofar as their promise can be measured.

At this point the Law School faced essentially three choices:

(1) It might admit the 275 applicants with the highest predicted first-year averages. This would produce the class with the greatest intellectual promise. It would also result in the admission of very few students from the four minority groups. Indeed, one consequence of the universal pursuit of this approach would be the admission of few minority students at the University of Washington or any other highly rated law school.

(2) The University of Washington Law School might seek only to rank applicants in terms of promise of law school success but give the LSAT tests and even college grades less weight in the case of minority applicants on

Board Ordinance', 71 Yale L.J. 1387 (1962); Navasky, 'The Benevolent Housing Quota', 6 Howard L.J. 30 (1960).

the not altogether unsupportable theory that the tests are biased against those who were not brought up in the traditional white culture. I regard this approach as somewhat disingenuous because it purports to forecast the relative academic promise of minorities without substituting for the scores and grades any other basis of prediction. It would, of course, increase the proportion of minority admissions.

(3) The University of Washington Law School might consciously determine to increase the number of students enrolled from the four minority groups by admitting them in preference to whites with higher prediction indices, provided that they seemed capable of adequate academic performance. This approach, if adopted generally, would increase the proportion of minority students at the best professional schools and presumably it would gradually raise the number of men and women belonging to minority groups who pursue the professional careers leading to positions of affluence and influence. It would also debar some students from the University of Washington Law School because they were white, whether Anglo-Saxon, Jew, or Italian, in the sense that if no racial preference had been given, they would have won by greater intellectual achievement some of the places actually going to members of the minorities.

Laying aside the Constitution for a moment, how *should* the University of Washington Law School deal with the problem? All applicants cannot be treated alike because there are not enough places even for those who meet the minimum qualifications. Give each individual the same opportunity to qualify, it may be said, without regard to race, creed, colour, sex, or national origin; this is the very essence of Equality. But what of the answer that the minority applicant does not have an opportunity 'equal' to the white's because the discriminatory denial of educational, professional, and cultural opportunities for generations past has severely handicapped him in any contest of early intellectual attainment? Do we achieve Equality by putting each individual on the same starting-line today or by giving minority applicants head-starts designed to offset the probable consequences of past discrimination and injustice against the group with which the applicant is identified?

One might plausibly answer that an institution of higher learning should concern itself only with intellectual performance and, in admissions, with the promise of the highest intellectual performance judged by the best available measures (aptitude scores and previous grades), because the use by a university of intellectual performance as the sole measure of excellence has enormous value in enhancing the quality of teaching and scholarship. Such use has also been important in reducing sundry invidious forms of rank and prejudice, first in higher education and then in the professions. The experience of the Jewish people in the United States is a good example.

But the argument does not run all one way even in educational terms. At Harvard College experience has convinced the Committee on Admissions that, given a high level of intellectual potential, the effectiveness of our undergraduates' educational experience is 'affected as importantly by a wide variety of interests, talents, backgrounds and career goals as it is by a fine faculty and . . . libraries, laboratories and housing arrangements'.[1] A student body will not reflect the rich diversity of contemporary America unless it includes substantial numbers of blacks, chicanos, and members of other identifiable minority groups. Even if one focuses exclusively on the classroom, education, including legal education, may be improved by including students whose experience and perceptions are affected by race. On one occasion a black student in my class in Constitutional Law spoke eloquently

[1] 65 Official Register of Harvard University No. 25, pp. 93, 104–5 (1968).

about the superiority of his education in a segregated school over the education of his younger brothers in an integrated school. His experience may have been unusual, but the point was worth making and only a black could make it effectively. The best education, moreover, looks to enlarging understanding and elevating the spirit as well as improving the intellect.

There is also a case to be made for setting educational objectives other than simply the best academic training for those with the most intellectual promise of professional competence and ability. Might not an institution of higher learning appropriately adopt as one of its objectives the lowering of the special obstacles facing disadvantaged minority groups needing access to higher education, business and professional opportunities, and professional services—obstacles which are the deeply ingrained consequences of the hostile public and private discrimination once pervading the entire social structure? I think so; but the rejoinder might be made that universities cannot be all things to all men, and we denigrate them by pursuing any goal other than scholarly accomplishment. And, attempting to compensate for past injustices by giving an arbitrary preference to any member of an entire minority group without regard to individual characteristics, upon the otherwise irrelevant criterion of race, may lead into the morass of permanent racial quotas and away from the ideal of equality of opportunity for individual accomplishment. In sum, there is weight to the arguments upon both sides.

The University of Washington chose to give a plus to minority applicants for law school admission. A number were admitted in preference to white students whose predicted academic performance was higher. One of the latter brought suit alleging that the University was an arm of the State, which was true; and that the State had violated the Fourteenth Amendment by engaging in racial discrimination. The case became moot before the Supreme Court could decide it.[1]

How *should* such a case be decided? Seen in one context the question is, what is the basic principle underlying the constitutional phrase 'equal protection of the laws'? Is the underlying principle that the State must be colour-blind or only that the electorate and its representatives, being predominantly white, may not engage in hostile or invidious discrimination against minorities of another colour? The Court's point of reference must be the constitutional guaranty of Equality, and a principled answer would reach beyond law school admissions. Still, seen in this light the question for the Court looks much like that facing the University of Washington Law School. Viewed from a different angle, the constitutional question is a variant of the problem discussed throughout these lectures: How much of the country's affairs should be handled as constitutional law? Should the Court substitute its judgment for the State educational authorities' judgment upon so difficult and debatable a question of educational policy? If leeway is to be allowed, the Court could formulate the conclusion in the language of the law by saying that only racial classifications *hostile* to a minority are subject to strict judicial scrutiny, and that others can pass if they are rationally related to a reasonable view of the public interest. The precedents sometimes stated the principle in broad language condemning all racial discrimination without a compelling justification, but in each the discrimination actually ran against the minority.[2]

There is much to be said for a rule requiring official colour-blindness. For the State to choose according to race introduces a peculiarly divisive element into the

---

[1] *De Funis* v. *Odegaard*, 416 U.S. 312 (1974), vacating 82 Wash. 2d 11, 507 P. 2d 1169 (1973).

[2] The precedents are best discussed in Ely, 'The Constitutionality of Reverse Racial Discrimination', 41 U. of Chi. L. Rev. 723 (1974).

community. The applicant excluded from the law school of his choice in favour of a minority applicant is likely to feel much more bitter than one excluded by reason of inferior, previous academic achievement. The State can hardly be a government of all the people in a nation of diverse origins unless it normally disregards race, creed, and colour. The long-range commitment expressed in the Equal Protection Clause is to a society that deems such factors irrelevant to the assessment of individual worth. Racial or ethnic preference even for the short term breeds notions of group entitlement based upon numbers instead of individual merit. There is no certain way of knowing just when the correctible disadvantages flowing from past invidious discrimination cease to operate. The danger that other ethnic groups—Italians, Poles, and Celts, for example—will allege that they too suffer like obstacles and should be given like preferences is very real.

It is risky to reply: 'It is a condition not a theory that confronts us.' Yet this threadbare academic saw summarizes the other side of the constitutional argument. The condition is the deeply ingrained obstacles that history put in the way of certain minorities' enjoyment of opportunities open to others. The wrongs done blacks, Orientals, American Indians, and, probably Chicanos, seem so much more severe as to be different in kind from those done to distinctive ethnic immigrants from Europe. Past denials of access to higher education and to executive, professional, and other intellectual occupations bred an outlook discouraging to youthful intellectual activity or achievement. Removing this disadvantage requires change in cultural background and visible opportunities. The decision to give a degree of preference to applicants from certain minority groups expresses the university's judgment that, once a certain level of academic ability is assured, the public and private interests served by using criteria measuring only intellectual competence are less important than the interests in making a demonstrably substantial effort to remove the obstacles clogging the access of plainly disadvantaged and identifiable groups to educational opportunities and professional careers; in bringing into education more of the diversity of American life; and in broadening the membership and vision of the legal profession and its capacity to give all segments of society understanding legal services. No one quite knows all the gains and costs of adopting such remedies instead of leaving the obstacles to diminish gradually once further discrimination is stopped.

Under these circumstances, I submit, the time for a rigid constitutional rule has not yet come. It is better to permit the State educational authorities to form their several individual judgments concerning the balance of educational and social advantage than to deny them freedom to attempt conscious remedies for past racial discrimination by the dominant whites.

IV

Chief Justice Warren regarded the Reapportionment Cases as the most important decisions of the decade and a half in which he presided over the Court. Malapportionment of legislative representatives had been a recurrent evil in many parts of the United States from the beginning. The grip of rural areas upon State legislatures tightened during the present century even as population was flowing to the cities. In some States the people of a rural county had as much as thirty-three times the *per capita* representation of a crowded city. A numerical majority in one or even both houses of a State legislature would be chosen by as little as twenty-five per cent of the people. The examples are extreme, but the vice was general.

It would have been best for the States themselves to act, but the rural legislators were more interested in self-perpetuation than electoral reform. Congress would not grasp the nettle. In theory, perhaps, unwillingness or inability to act on the part of the political branches of government cannot enlarge the jurisdiction of the federal judicial branch, but as a practicality there is, and I suspect has to be, a good deal of play in the joints. Much of the activism of the Warren Court flowed from the neglect of other agencies of government. In *Baker* v. *Carr*[1] the Court launched the judiciary into the political thicket by holding that justiciable controversy is presented by an allegation that a State is apportioning seats in its legislature without regard to equal representation *per capita* and without justification for the departures, in violation of its constitutional obligation not to 'deny any person . . . equal protection of the laws'. In *Reynolds* v. *Sims*[2] the Court held that 'as a basic constitutional standard the Equal Protection Clause requires that the seats in both houses of a bicameral state legislature must be apportioned on a population basis'. The same rule was laid down for the U.S. House of Representatives.[3] By these 'one man, one vote' decisions the Court removed the chief remaining source of political inequality in the United States and gave impetus to other correctives.

v

The successful accomplishment of such major reforms by constitutional litigation led other groups to invoke the Equal Protection Clause in an effort to obtain by adjudication what they could not win in the political arena. The civil rights cases set up a classification of especially 'invidious' discriminations which were unconstitutional, if not absolutely, then in the absence of some extraordinary justification. Could not the Court be persuaded

[1] 369 U.S. 186 (1962).   [2] 377 U.S. 533 (1964).
[3] *Wesbury* v. *Saunders*, 376 U.S. 1 (1964).

to put in this special category statutory distinctions based upon legitimacy of birth, marital status, citizenship, length of residence, sex, wealth or indigency, etc.? The reapportionment cases had required the Court to make another kind of exception to the general rule of judicial tolerance for rational legislative classifications. Any number of relevant considerions could be cited to justify giving some geographical constituencies greater *per capita* representation than others: economic importance, geographical size, offsetting the weight of urban bloc voting, etc. Nor could the lines of differentiation be called 'invidious'. In justifying strict scrutiny the Court observed:

Undoubtedly, the right of suffrage is a fundamental matter in a free and democratic society. Especially since the right to exercise the franchise in a free and unimpaired manner is preservative of other basic civil and political rights, any alleged infringement of the right of citizens to vote must be carefully and meticulously scrutinized.[1]

The category of 'fundamental rights' looked capable of expansion. In a much earlier case the Court had held an Oklahoma statute to violate the Equal Protection Clause because it provided for the sterilization of criminals convicted of felonies three or more times. The line between felonies and misdemeanours was too arbitrary for use in this context, the Court held; 'we are dealing here with legislation which involves one of the fundamental rights of man . . . strict scrutiny of a classification which a State makes in a sterilization law is essential . . .'[2] If strict scrutiny is appropriate for classifications in voting and sterilization laws, why not in laws dealing with public welfare, hospital care, public housing, education, and like necessities?

[1] *Reynolds* v. *Sims*, 377 U.S. 533, 56 1–2 (1964).
[2] *Skinner* v. *Oklahoma*, 316 U.S. 535, 541 (1942).

The next two important cases encouraged the propo-
nents of these two lines of constitutional development.
Harper v. *Board of Elections* held unconstitutional a State
statute making a payment of a modest poll tax a condition
of eligibility to vote. 'Lines drawn on the basis of wealth
or property like those of race . . . are traditionally dis-
favored . . . To introduce wealth or payment of a fee as a
measure of a voter's qualifications is to introduce a
capricious or irrelevant factor.'[1]

Shapiro v. *Thompson*[2] invalidated State laws requiring
one year's prior residency to qualify for State welfare
payments to indigent mothers with dependent children.
Some passages in the opinion seemed to put the decision
upon the ground that discrimination based upon exercise
of the privilege of interstate movement is especially
'invidious'. Elsewhere the majority intimated that receipt
of welfare payments when indigent is a 'fundamental
right'.

Later decisions subject other residency requirements to
strict scrutiny, invalidating some while approving others.[3]
In another series of decisions the Court invalidated sundry
restrictions upon voting rights.[4] Still other opinions held
statutory classifications to be unconstitutional, because
invidious and lacking compelling justification, where

[1] *Harper* v. *Board of Elections*, 383 U.S. 663, 668 (1966).

[2] 394 U.S. 618 (1969).

[3] *Dunn* v. *Blumstein*, 405 U.S. 330 (1972) (one year prior residence unconstitutional requirement for voting); *Marston* v. *Lewis*, 410 U.S. 679 (1973)
(50 day prior residence requirement constitutional for voting); *Memorial Hospital*
v. *Maricopa County*, 415 U.S. 250 (1974) (one year prior residency requirement
unconstitutional as applied to free hospital care of indigent); *Starns* v. *Malkerson*,
326 F. Supp. 234, affirmed, 401 U.S. 985 (1971) (tuition preference for in-State
students at State university constitutional).

[4] *Kramer* v. *Union Free School District* No. 15, 395 U.S. 621 (1969) (unconstitutional to limit vote in school board elections to parents of children and
owners and lessees of real property); *Cipriano* v. *City of Houma*, 395 U.S. 701
(1969) (unconstitutional to restrict voting on a municipal bond issue to property
owners); *Richardson* v. *Ramirez*, 418 U.S. 24 (1974) (constitutional to dis-
enfranchise ex-felons).

based upon alienage[1] or illegitimacy of birth.[2] Distinctions based upon sex have also been held to violate the Equal Protection Clause but without putting them yet in a class for strict scrutiny.[3]

Nearly all the cases provoked sharp dispute between the relatively conservative Justices and the activists believing in vigorous use of the Equal Protection Clause as a vehicle for expanding the use of constitutional adjudication as an instrument of reform. It is not necessary to trace the debate through the numerous opinions,[4] but three observations may be helpful.

First, the questions of judicial philosophy which these cases raise are the same as those posed when the Due Process Clause is invoked to protect personal liberties not specifically mentioned in the Bill of Rights.[5] When and how far is the Court to substitute its judgment for that of the political branches? When is it to investigate conditions for itself? When is it to defer to implied legislative findings? There is one marked difference. The Fourteenth Amendment embodies a mandate of 'equal' treatment by all branches of government which has more undeniable substantive content than the concept of 'due process of law'. Under the Equal Protection Clause the judicial task is inescapably one of drawing lines, preferably in terms of general, enduring principle. Under the Due Process Clause it is possible to stand aside when procedural fairness has been satisfied, or to confine any substantive protection to the specifics of the Bill of Rights. Since the

---

[1] *Graham* v. *Richardson*, 403 U.S. 365 (1971); In re Griffiths, 413 U.S. 717 (1973).

[2] *Weber* v. *Aetna Casualty & Surety Co.*, 406 U.S. 164 (1972).

[3] *Reed* v. *Reed*, 404 U.S. 71 (1971); *Frontiero* v. *Richardson*, 411 U.S. 677 (1973).

[4] Fuller discussions will be found in Gunther, 'The Supreme Court, 1971 Term: Forward', 86 Harv. L. Rev. 1 (1972); Karst, 'Invidious Discrimination: Justice Douglas and the Return of the "Natural Law—Due Process" Formula', 16 U.C.L.A. L. Rev. 716 (1969).

[5] See pp. 31–36 above.

Court has not thus confined itself, the tasks today are much alike.

Second, although the use of the 'strict scrutiny' formula for cases involving 'invidious' classifications or differentiations in access to a 'fundamental right' has been checked, the Justices have been notably unsuccessful in formulating viable general principles explaining their votes and imparting a measure of consistency to their decisions. The earmarks of 'invidious' go undescribed although there are suggestions that the term applies only to discrimination against 'discrete insular minorities'. Justice Powell, in an opinion of the Court, stated that the only fundamental rights for the purpose of the Equal Protection Clause are those 'implicitly or explicitly guaranteed by the Constitution'.[1] The cases hardly fit this Procrustean bed. Only the Equal Protection Clause protects the right to vote. The right to procreation and abortion are protected by the Equal Protection and Due Process Clauses only because the Court chose thus to recognize them.

The decisions also seem curiously inconsistent (although the want of a yardstick makes this an essentially personal, impressionistic appraisal). Congress, the Court has held, may grant payments for educational purposes to young men who have been required to serve in the armed forces under the Selective Service Act, while withholding like payments from young men who had been required to serve in hospitals and similar public institutions for the same period, having been excused from service in the armed forces by reason of religious conscientious objection to military service in any war. Although both groups were wrenched out of their normal activities and forced to forgo further education at the age when young people usually pursue it, as integral parts of a programme for building up the armed forces, Congress was allowed to make the judgment that differences in the degree of

[1] San Antonio Independent School District v. Rodriguez, 411 U.S. 1, 33 (1973).

separation from normal civilian activities, in difficulty of readjustment, and in effect upon the morale of the armed forces called for paying benefits to one class but not the other.[1] In another case the Court held that Congress may not constitutionally withhold from married women in the armed forces the allowances made to married men.[2] Evidently Congress had made the judgment that there were more and better reasons for taking steps to encourage the traditional family relationship under which the wife maintains the home and takes care of any children than there were to enlarge the income of a wife. Why was one judgment treated as suitable for the political branches but not the other? By what criteria can one judgment be held so wrongheaded that the judiciary must intervene while the other is allowed? If there is any helpless, political minority, surely it is conscientious objectors and not women.

Consider a second pair of decisions. In *Eisenstadt* v. *Baird*[3] the Supreme Court held that Massachusetts could not constitutionally prohibit the sale of contraceptives to unmarried persons while allowing sales to married persons having a physician's prescription. An earlier statute prohibited all sales of contraceptives. Obviously the legislature judged it undesirable to vote a measure removing one of the deterrents to sexual intercourse among unmarried persons. In another case the Court upheld a statute which put a ceiling upon welfare payments to a single family regardless of need, thus discriminating against children in large families.[4] In effect, it deferred to a legislative judgment that providing the same minimum level of subsistence to children in large families as in small is less important than preserving a

---

[1] *Johnson* v. *Robison*, 415 U.S. 361 (1974).
[2] *Frontiero* v. *Richardson*, 411 U.S. 677 (1973).
[3] 405 U.S. 438 (1972).
[4] *Dandridge* v. *Williams*, 397 U.S. 471 (1970).

proper relationship between welfare payments and earnings at the minimum wage. Again, it is hard to find a principle that allows a legislature to form the second judgment but not the first, unless it be that the Constitution now prohibits a legislature from acting upon the basis of an old-fashioned morality.

I do not mean to leave the impression that difficulty in formulating decisional standards or even inconsistency in results is enough to condemn all recent developments under the Equal Protection Clause. My points are much narrower. First, the effort to articulate principles is worth pursuing because the ability to rationalize decisions in terms of conventional sources of law is one of the sources of public acceptance and support. Second, inconsistency and eclecticism in minor cases suggests that the Court is venturing essentially political judgments which may fritter away resources better reserved for great occasions.

IV

THE AFFIRMATIVE DUTIES
OF GOVERNMENT

THROUGHOUT most of our history the form of the Supreme Court's contributions to public policy was negative. To note this aspect is not to minimize the importance of Chief Justice Marshall's grand conception of a politically and economically unified Nation, the influence of the Court's great opinions upon the national consciousness, the momentum generated by important judgments legitimating assertions of State or congressional power, or the obvious fact that eliminating a governmental restraint upon private action may release forces that do more to shape the character of life than any governmental measure. The work was done, however, in the process of rendering judgments which did little more than validate or veto allegedly unconstitutional action by other branches of government: by the President, by the President and Congress, by the States and the State legislatures, governors and courts, and by other minor officials. Decrees telling State officials what programme they should institute and requiring legislatures to appropriate vast sums would have been unthinkable. When the Court entered its validation or veto, it was done with the matter.

Under the Warren Court this proposition ceased to be

true. Some of its most important decisions mandated reforms in the current activities of other branches of government. Reforms often require affirmative action. The affirmative action can be secured only through voluntary co-operation of the political branches or by the courts embarking upon programmes having typically administrative, executive, and even legislative characteristics heretofore thought to make the activity unsuited to judicial undertaking. This new dimension of constitutional adjudication raises questions concerning the proper role of the Supreme Court in American government on which past experience and studies shed little light.

I. AFFIRMATIVE REMEDIES

School Desegregation

When the Supreme Court ruled that segregation of children in the public schools according to race or colour violated the Equal Protection Clause of the Fourteenth Amendment, it implied that the constitutional rights of black children had been continuously violated in the old South for half a century. The question then became: what should be the remedy? The answer has been to require 'desegregation' by judicial decree. The answer requires the courts to formulate controversial programmes of affirmative action requiring detailed administration for protracted periods under constant judicial supervision. In major metropolitan areas the court decrees that require extensive busing in order to achieve racially balanced schools have all the qualities of social legislation: they pertain to the future; they are mandatory; they govern millions of people; they reorder people's lives in ways that benefit some and disappoint others in order to achieve social objectives. I can think of no earlier decrees with these characteristics in all our constitutional history. Because of the challenge to judicial competence, and also because some points of legal principle are still unsettled, the problem deserves exposition in some detail.

One source of uncertainty is the ambiguity of the Supreme Court's pronouncements. The initial opinion in *Brown* v. *Board of Education* ruled that

segregation of children in public schools solely on the basis of race even though the physical facilities and other tangible factors may be equal, deprive[s] the children of the minority group of equal educational opportunities.

Separate educational facilities are inherently unequal.[1]

A later opinion dealing with the relief to be awarded for past violations spoke of the State's duty to bring about a 'transition to a system freed of racial discrimination'.[2]

The ambiguity in these declarations has caused continuous difficulty. The abstract noun 'segregation' could mean either the act of segregating or the condition of having black children in some schools and white children in others. The sentence, 'Separate educational facilities are inherently unequal', points towards the latter reading. If it be the rule, the Constitution itself requires the States and school districts which provide public education to provide it in racially integrated schools; and each must find some way to arrange for integration. On the other hand, 'segregation' might mean only assigning children to schools according to race. Then the legal situation is quite different. At a minimum the acts of racial segregation must be stopped. Further relief might be thought appropriate where the prior unconstitutional acts had consequences which could be remedied only by providing integrated education, but otherwise there would be no duty to provide integrated education. One can readily summon up other possible variations upon these themes.

A second source of difficulty is the endless variety of

[1] 347 U.S. 483, 493, 495 (1954).   [2] 349 U.S. 294, 299 (1955).

situations with which the courts must deal. The conventional unit of school financing and administration in the United States is the self-governing school district, which usually conforms to the boundaries of a city, town, county, or other local political subdivision of a State. Their variety can be suggested by four examples.

In a rural, Southern school district black families and white families often live interspersed over the whole area. In one such case there were two schools, one at each end of the district. Under segregation, one school was for black children, the other for white. Some children may have lived close enough to walk to the assigned school, but others were taken to school each morning in school buses and taken home each afternoon. When required to desegregate, the School Board adopted a rule permitting every child to attend whichever school he wished. A few black children chose to go to the white school, but otherwise the situation continued as before. The momentum of the previous violations of the Equal Protection Clause continued to brand one school 'white' and the other 'black' as unmistakably as if signs still hung upon the doors. The Supreme Court held that giving students freedom of choice was not sufficient—that the school board must take further affirmative steps to establish a 'unitary system'.[1] The proper application of the decree seems clear enough. Children living at one end of the county should be assigned the former white school regardless of race; children living at the other end of the county should be assigned the former black school regardless of race. Segregation and also, one might hope, the momentum from past segregation, would be eliminated.

In metropolitan areas in the North the schools are scattered in such a way that the overwhelming proportion of all children live within walking distance and go to

[1] *Green* v. *New Kent County School Board*, 391 U.S. 430 (1968).

school with their neighbours. Housing often follows economic and racial patterns. The result was that most children went to schools which were overwhelmingly black, or overwhelmingly white, without any legally enforced segregation; indeed this situation could well develop in a school district in which none of the decisions concerning school assignments or even school location had been influenced by racial considerations. After years of the uncertainty the Supreme Court indicated that this condition (which Americans describe by the barbaric phrase *de facto* segregation') does not violate the Fourteenth Amendment.[1]

Transplant the metropolitan school district just described to a city in one of the old slave-holding States. Before *Brown* a State statute would have made segregation mandatory. Some pupil assignments would be dictated by race. Racial considerations would influence decisions concerning whether, when, and where to construct additional classrooms. The school system might have influenced racial patterns in housing. In such a case the cessation of active segregation and other colour-conscious practices and the substitution of colour-blind assignment to neighbourhood schools would not result in integrated education. Hence the question would arise: is some further remedy required for the previous unconstitutional action? In Charlotte, N.C., a federal district judge concluded that a 'unitary school system' could be established under these circumstances only by assigning pupils to schools some distance from their homes, taking black children in the urban centre out toward the wealthier suburbs and white children from the suburbs in to the centre so as to integrate all the district's schools. The assignments could be carried out only by large scale busing. The Supreme Court of the United States held that

[1] *Swann* v. *Charlotte-Mecklenburg Board of Education*, 402 U.S. 1, 28 (1971); *Keyes* v. *School District*, 413 U.S. 189 (1973) (semble).

the district court had not abused its discretion to frame an appropriate remedy.[1]

Consider for a last example a case from Detroit, Michigan, not long since decided by the Supreme Court.[2] It is not typical because it involved much the largest numbers of pupils, buses, and school districts yet to come before a court. I choose the example partly because the opinion is the latest judicial exposition of the legal principles and partly because the case's gigantic scale underscores general characteristics common to nearly all urban cases.

In 1970 an overwhelming proportion of Detroit's 290,000 school children attended schools in which the pupils were virtually all black or virtually all white. The U.S. District Court found that the Detroit school authorities had engaged in various acts of discrimination contributing to this condition: (i) some attendance zones were laid out to conform to racial residential boundaries; (ii) particular grade schools were designated to 'feed' particular high schools so as to facilitate racial segregation; (iii) optional attendance zones were sometimes created to enable white students to leave a school where the proportion of black students had increased; (iv) on occasion, when overcrowding required the transportation of black students beyond their immediate residential area, they were carried beyond a white school to a black school; and (v) decisions concerning school construction were sometimes shaped to facilitate segregation. The State of Michigan contributed to the segregation by refusing to make the same financial allowances for transportation in Detroit as in other parts of Michigan and by forbidding the Detroit School Board to assign pupils away from the nearest available neighbourhood school. The Federal Housing Authority and also the Veterans Administration were found for a number

---

[1] *Swann* v. *Charlotte-Mecklenburg Board of Education*, 402 U.S. 1 (1971).
[2] *Milliken* v. *Bradley*, 418 U.S. 717 (1974).

of years prior to 1948 to have advocated the maintenance of racially and economically 'harmonious' neighbourhoods, thus putting their official influence behind economic class and racial discrimination by real estate brokers, financial institutions, landlords, and developers in the financing and sales of residential housing.

The district court ruled that these official practices violated the Fourteenth Amendment, and that it was therefore its duty to integrate the Detroit schools. Finding this impossible without drawing upon the white children in suburbs, the court made 53 additional school districts part of the desegregation area, thereby raising the number of pupils involved from 290,000 to approximately 750,000. The order subdivided the total area into so-called 'clusters', each with a school population the racial mixture of which was equal to the mixture of the total area. Children were to be assigned to schools within a cluster in such a way that 'no school, grade or classroom be substantially disproportionate to overall pupil racial composition'. The opinion and order speak of limits upon travel time, but observe that 'upwards of one hour, and up to one and one half hours, one way on the bus ride to school will not endanger the health or safety of the children nor impinge on the education process'. Transportation was to be a two-way process with black and white pupils sharing equally.

The decree also required 'restructuring school facility utilization' to produce schools of 'like quality, facilities, extra-curricular activities and staffs'. In faculty assignments 'the desideratum is the balance of faculty and staff by qualifications for subject and grade level, and then by race, experience and sex'. Affirmative action is to be taken in order 'to increase minority employment at all levels'. The factor of racial balance was to be considered 'along with other educational considerations' in constructing and expanding school facilities. Such provisions are necessary, fair, and wise. The striking point, however, is that they invite bringing into court before a federal judge all the thousands of disputes bound to arise in any large school system in the course of implementing the soundest of racial, educational, construction, and personnel policies; for anyone disappointed by an administrative decision can easily allege that it fails to comply with the court's decree. Consider, for example, the potential for controversy and the intense feelings likely to be generated in an area as racially and ethnically diversified as Greater Detroit by a dispute over whether 'the curriculum, activities, and conduct standards respect the diversity of students from different ethnic backgrounds and the dignity and safety of each individual, students, faculty, staff and parents.'

The bringing in of fifty-three additional school districts produced problems of still another dimension. Who was to govern school affairs in the segregation area? Who was to employ the teachers? What were to be the financial arrangements? The disposition of property? The method of funding capital expenditure and paying off earlier bond issues? Whence would a court get the competence to decide such questions?

In the summer of 1974 the Supreme Court set this decree aside upon a 5–4 vote on the ground that it was improper to include the fifty-three outside school districts in the plan of desegregation because they had not violated the Fourteenth Amendment. The ruling will substantially curtail racial integration in Northern school systems. In cities like Detroit, where the school population is overwhelmingly black, there will be no way for a federal court to bring about a racial balance. In a number of other cities where blacks preponderate but substantial numbers of whites remain, civil rights groups will be deterred from bringing suit to vindicate their constitutional rights by the fear of causing more and more white families to move out of the white suburbs with their own independent school districts. The flight also lessens the effectiveness of decrees which have been entered.

Whether the Detroit case will have still further consequences depends upon the theoretical underpinning of the ruling that the fifty-three suburban school districts should not have been included in a plan for integration because none of them had individually joined in violating the Constitution. Much of the opinion is devoted to explaining that their autonomy is too valuable to sacrifice to the interest in providing integrated education as a remedy for wrongs in Detroit. If the problem is indeed one of balancing gains against costs and the cost of sacrificing local autonomy is the decisive factor, the decision will have no precedential value in ruling upon remedies confined to an offending school district. But to say that a balance must be struck neither explains why nor supplies a rule of decision. In another part of the opinion Chief Justice Burger seemed to take as his major premise the fundamental principle that a judicial remedy should be limited to what will 'restore the victims of discriminatory conduct to the position they would have occupied in the absence of such conduct'.[1] This principle seems applicable to single district cases and can be applied in a way that would greatly limit the use of busing and other affirmative measures for achieving racial integration. Whether the principle will be so applied depends intellectually upon what the Court meant by 'the position they would have occupied in the absence' of unconstitutional discrimination. The opinion of the Court gives no explanation. Justice Stewart essayed an explanation tucked away in a footnote in a concurring opinion:

It is this essential fact of a predominantly Negro school population in Detroit—caused by unknown and perhaps unknowable factors such as in-migration, birth rates, economic changes, or cumulative acts of private racial fears—that accounts for the 'growing core of

[1] Id. at 746.

Negro schools'; a core that has grown to include virtually the entire city. The Constitution simply does not allow federal courts to attempt to change that situation unless and until it is shown that the State, or its political sub-divisions, have contributed to cause the situation to exist.[1]

Justice White, who dissented, took a broader view:

the Court's remedy will not restore to the Negro community, stigmatized as it was by the dual school system, what it would have enjoyed over all or most of this period if the remedy is confined to present-day Detroit. . . . The education of children of different races in a desegregated environment has unhappily been lost, along with the social, economic and political advantages which accompany a desegregated system as compared with an unconstitutionally segregated system.[2]

One wishes that the dialogue had proceeded further. Presumably Justice White would agree that, given the actual history of race relations in the United States, today's Detroit school children would almost surely be going to all-black schools even if there had never been unconstitutional discrimination in Detroit. Surely Justice Stewart would then have pressed Justice White to concede that the social, economic, and political disadvantages of that not unconstitutional condition would be very little different from the social, economic, and political disadvantages to which Justice White referred. Perhaps Justice White would have replied by widening the focus of the discussion. He might have argued that one cannot look merely to what would have happened in Detroit without violation of the Constitution, given the actual history of race relations in the United States, because that history itself was a mass of unconstitutional action all over the country; and that the courts must seek to create the social, economic, and political conditions that would have developed in the absence of unconstitutional action anywhere and assume that other violations in other

[1] Id. at 756.   [2] Id. at 779–80.

communities are being remedied by other decrees requiring school integration. Had the dialogue gone this far
we would at least have learned what the individual Justices
conceive to be the ultimate premises of the remedies they
advocate. And the full scope of what some of the Justices
are trying to accomplish would be apparent.

If the principle is that busing and other complex and
far-reaching remedies designed to give every student
education in an integrated school need not be prescribed
where it appears likely that today's black students would
be attending overwhelmingly black schools even if the
Constitution had never been violated in that particular
district, then the decision is logically no less applicable
to a single school district (such as Charlotte, North
Carolina). Probably, the Detroit opinion can be read
either way in the future, according to the will of a majority
of the Justices. For the present, however, we must take
it that the Detroit decree would have been not only within
judicial discretion but required if all the city and suburban
schools had been within the same school district. In a
1973 case from Denver, Colorado, the proof showed
racial discrimination in a very small part of the city, but
the schools in other parts were overwhelmingly white,
black, or chicano, according to the residential pattern.
The six-man majority declared that 'the School Board has
the affirmative duty to desegregate the entire school
system "root and branch" '. Once again, unhappily, the
Court vouchsafed no reasons.[1]

I deal at length with the school desegregation cases
because it is plain that in undertaking to wipe out the
consequences of past violations of the Fourteenth Amendment in public school education, the federal courts have
taken on altogether novel and overwhelming tasks in the
name of 'constitutional adjudication' that subject the
institution to strains never before experienced. One

---

[1] *Keyes* v. *School District*, 413 U.S. 189, 213 (1973).

novel aspect is the affirmative character of the remedies
judicially prescribed. Second, the necessary components
of any programme of integrated education in a large city
appear to commit the courts to constant executive or
administrative supervision of the organization, employment practices, curriculum, and extra-curricular activities
of the entire Detroit school system. Third, desegregation
decrees have all the qualities of social legislation. They
pertain to the future. They are mandatory, they govern
millions of people. They reorder people's lives in a way
that benefits some and disappoints others in order to
achieve social objectives. Many of the parents whose
children are to be bused into other neighbourhoods
pursued the ambition of moving to a 'better neighbourhood' not alone or even primarily for their own lives,
but for what they saw as a preferable social life and better
education of their children. The decrees directing the
State to remove children from this environment not only
frustrate the parent's aspirations but, as the parents often
see it, threaten the emotional well-being and possibly the
physical safety of their children. There must be many
parents in the inner cities who share very similar mis-
givings about the government's 'pushing their children
around' by assigning them to schools in the so-called
'better' neighbourhoods. The decrees thus directly regulate the lives of millions of people without voice in the
decision.

I can think of no earlier decrees with these characteristics
in all constitutional history. Apart from the unhappy
experience with economic 'due process', constitutional
adjudication under both the Fourteenth Amendment and
the Bill of Rights has been concerned with stopping
wrongs done by a State to a few individuals or a minority
—usually by official aggression but sometimes, recently,
by withholding benefits or other public protection. The
economic due process decisions did involve the accom-

modation of the conflicting interests of large social and economic classes, but even there the Court was vetoing accommodations worked out through the political process, not imposing upon millions of people a novel programme of legislative character without popular representation. They were wrong primarily because the Justices in the majority failed to perceive the changes in American society, but one wonders whether they were not also wrong in thinking that issues involving the accommodation of the direct interests of large groups of people are fit for judicial resolution.

These characteristics of the school desegregation decrees are typical of legislative action. In emphasizing this fact I do not mean to imply that the courts should have omitted the undertaking. Quite likely it was the only way to instil conviction that the constitutional promise of equality was genuine and capable of realization. But approval of the aim and even of the means chosen should not blind us either to the novel aspects of the judicial venture or to the resulting degree of judicial dependence upon political support. The courts cannot possibly go it alone. At the very minimum the community's professional educators must co-operate. Even that will hardly do if the political community withholds its support and the people are recalcitrant. The danger is not inconsiderable because these quasi-legislative decrees cannot be said, like true legislation, to have the legitimacy which flows from the processes of democratic self-government.

One sees the consequences at their worst in the violence, hatreds, and frustration consequent upon the effort to integrate previously segregated schools in Boston. Part of the city is an extraordinarily homogeneous, proud and self-conscious Irish Roman Catholic community, politically powerful in eastern Massachusetts yet in many ways isolated and inward-looking, perhaps because of earlier decades of discrimination against the Irish because of their race and religion. As a whole this South Boston community has not shared the affluence of the suburbs. Perhaps some of its members fear the upward movement of the black people of the neighbouring Roxbury district from the bottom of the economic ladder, especially into the building trades and the fire and police departments, as a further threat to their economic well-being. Although Boston had escaped the riots which occurred in a number of cities there was occasional violence along the fringes. Worst of all, too many local politicians had run too long for the School Committee and other local offices upon the promise that Boston's schools would never be integrated; and such are the delays of reform through litigation that integration was indeed held off until the autumn of 1974. The result was an outbreak of fear, frustration, and violence, which is still disruptive.

It would be wrong to think of Boston as anything but an extreme instance. In the South seventy-five per cent of all black pupils are now attending schools with a large white enrolment. In the North roughly half of all black pupils attend truly integrated schools. The figure from the North is much smaller partly because of the 'de facto segregation' resulting from housing patterns, partly because in some entire school districts the school population is overwhelmingly black, and partly because the leaders of the black communities in some cities have not brought or not strongly supported law suits asking the courts to require integration. Measured by the goal, the changes took too long, and little enough has been accomplished. Measured by the conditions of 1954, the dream of justice and equality in race relations by the affirmative intervention of the courts has been to some extent realized.

The mixed picture is a reminder that reforms in the social order, while promoted by constitutional adjudication, cannot be won by judicial decree alone. For half a decade after *Brown* there was no significant executive or legislative support for school desegregation, and progress was halting under judicial decree. From 1961 to 1969 integration progressed faster because the political branches gave varying measures of effective support in the area of education in addition to enacting legislation striking at discriminatory racial practices in such related fields as housing, employment, voting and public accommodations. After 1969 resistance became stiffer and compliance slowed while President Nixon pressed for legislation to deprive the courts of power to remedy past denials of Equal Protection through the affirmative programmes described above. The issue became a symbol not only of basic attitudes towards the struggle for racial equality but also in terms of constitutionalism, for the measures, if enacted, would have put the legislative branch in the position of attempting to limit the power of the judiciary to frame remedies pursuant to its constitutional adjudications.

Reapportionment

The Reapportionment Cases, although much less controversial, provide a second dramatic example of judicial involvement in affirmative undertakings of an essentially legislative character as a consequence of constitutional adjudication. The Equal Protection Clause was held to require seats in elected legislative bodies to be apportioned equally *per capita* among geographical districts: 'one man, one vote'.[1] In theory, if an apportionment is shown to violate the standard, a court can content itself with declaring the existing system invalid and forbidding future elections until the system is reformed. As a practical matter, to hold no elections would be intolerable. If the legislature does not act, the court must take the affirmative step of preparing a new apportionment. A statistician using a computer could produce for any State

[1] See pp. 68–9 above.

scores of apportionment plans conforming to the one man, one vote rule. The choice between constitutionally adequate plans depends upon altogether different questions: (a) how many 'safe' districts shall be created for the major parties; (b) should the bias be towards protecting incumbents or pitting them against each other; (c) which party will be favoured; (d) shall an area heavily populated by a self-conscious racial or ethnic minority be made a single district, in which case it may elect one truly representative figure, or shall it be divided, in which case the minority may, under some circumstances, lose all power but, under other circumstances, exert decisive influence in two or three districts; (e) should the district lines follow existing municipal and county lines; (f) how much use should be made of multi-member districts? The answers have large political consequences. Judges can devise the plans, if they have to do it, calling upon expert assistance, but they do not like the assignment because a court's public stature depends upon both the appearance and actuality of freedom from electoral politics, and because there are no legal principles to govern the choice among constitutional plans. The task is utterly unlike any previously thought appropriate for a court, but it has been performed with apparent success by a number of State and federal judges.[1]

II. AFFIRMATIVE DUTIES

In the school desegregation and reapportionment cases the affirmative judicial decrees with quasi-legislative qualities were entered as remedies for past violations of constitutional prohibitions. Other cases indicate that the Due Process and Equal Protection Clauses are themselves becoming sources of individual and group constitutional

[1] Dixon, *Democratic Representation: Reapportionment in Law and Politics* (1968), pp. 291–329.

rights to have the government perform affirmative duties. Simple examples are in *Griffin* v. *Illinois*[1] and *Douglas* v. *California*,[2] holding that a State must provide an indigent person charged with crime with funds to buy a transcript of the evidence at the trial and to retain a lawyer for appeal. Formerly allegations of denial of equal protection were focused upon the sanctions a State was imposing upon one group but not another. Today the charge more often is that the State is failing to provide equal benefits: in welfare, in education, in municipal protection. Formerly, one would have regarded the Due Process Clause as a check upon the government's power to push people around. Today, the clause is sometimes a basis for obtaining benefits such as medical care and job training in penitentiaries, and education in institutions for retarded children.

The most ambitious effort to use the Constitution to reform on-going State programmes by imposing new affirmative duties came in the area of school finance. In most of our States the cost of public elementary and secondary education is financed chiefly by an *ad valorem* property tax levied by each local school district upon the real and personal property within its jurisdiction. In Texas, where the case that went to the Supreme Court arose, about half the cost was thus financed. Enormous disparities developed in the taxable value of the property in different districts, and thus in the wealth per pupil. These disparities were reflected in wide differences among districts in expenditures per pupil for public education. The last set of differences, it was argued, amounted to 'invidious' classification upon grounds of wealth and also related to a 'fundamental right' because the interest in education should be classed as fundamental. For either reason, or both, the argument concluded, the difference in the value of the education offered the pupils in different

[1] 351 U.S. 12 (1956).   [2] 372 U.S. 353 (1963).

districts should be held to violate the Equal Protection Clause.

Three aspects of the school-finance litigation are characteristic of the new dimensions of much constitutional litigation:

(1) The suit looked to judicial reform of long-established practices prevailing in virtually every State.

(2) The constitutional claim depended upon group comparisons, asserted a group right, and would have reordered the distribution of tax burdens and revenue benefits among various groups. The State was not classifying individuals in terms of wealth.

(3) The complainants were not seeking to prevent a State from intruding on their right to be left alone, or from regulating their conduct without observing procedural safeguards; they were saying that the State was not operating its educational system in the way which the complainants wished and that it should be required to operate the system differently. The issue concerned the on-going performance of an affirmative State programme. The decree, if the complainants prevailed, would prescribe affirmatively the manner in which the State's duty should be performed.

The Supreme Court rejected the constitutional arguments, five to four.[1] Justice Powell's opinion puts the greatest emphasis upon the absence of individual classification according to wealth and upon the State's provision of some education for every child. In terms of constitutional formulas he rejects strict review upon the ground that the classification is not 'invidious' and education is not a 'fundamental right'. These elements and the underlying issues concerning the reach of the Equal Protection Clause undoubtedly carried weight, but I am inclined to think that the decisive factor was the Court's scarcely expressed worry about the difficulty of the judiciary's

---

[1] *San Antonio Independent School District* v. *Rodriguez*, 411 U.S. 1 (1973).

laying upon communities essentially affirmative, on-going obligations for the benefit of disadvantaged groups.

Pause for a moment to transport the imagination into an altogether different world. Suppose that all 50 States had always financed the public schools entirely out of state-wide revenues allocated among local school districts on a per pupil basis. Suppose further that a single State decided to substitute local financing based upon local property taxes, and that the differences in tax base among school districts were as large as those revealed in *Rodriguez*. Would not the *new* State law be held to violate the Equal Protection Clause because it introduced patently arbitrary and capricious differentiations into public education—differentiations not required to achieve local autonomy and responsibility? My instinct is that this would be the decision by a heavy majority, if not unanimous, vote of the Court. Yet in the actual case the Court upheld the differentiation.

One difference between the imaginary situation and the actual case is that the actual suit looked to the reform of a long-established practice prevailing in forty-nine States, but the abortion cases indicate that this alone might not have had great influence. The greater difference is in the posture in which a ruling of unconstitutionality would leave the Court. In our imaginary world a ruling of unconstitutionality would have led to an injunction categorically forbidding named officials from doing the specific acts involved in putting the new statute into effect; the status quo would continue, and the judicial work would be done. Given the actual case, anyone proposing a ruling of unconstitutionality would be hard put to it to answer the question: what happens next?

Ideally, the legislatures would promptly set up new methods of financing primary and secondary education. Each would face extraordinarily difficult questions of tax and fiscal policy. Should public school education be centrally financed out of State revenues? Or should the State adopt the ingenious 'district power-equalization' scheme, under which a district with a tax base per pupil above the State-wide average would contribute part of the school revenues it chose to raise to districts whose tax base per pupil was below the State-wide average? A third possibility might be to redraw school district lines to equalize the tax bases. A fourth would be to remove commercial, industrial, and mineral property from the local tax rolls, tax this property State-wide and use the proceeds to equalize inequalities resulting from the disparities in the remaining local tax bases. From a constitutional standpoint it would not matter what choice was made. The first question the Court would have to worry about would be—will the judicial mandate impel the legislatures of forty-nine States to appropriate action?

Perhaps it would; but surely the strain upon the authority of the Court is greater than that created by the traditional decree forbidding a named official from interfering with private individuals or businesses in a specified manner. It would be hardly surprising if some legislature failed to act out of stubbornness, inability to reach a consensus among its members, or a despairing willingness, as in some reapportionment cases, to dump its problems upon the court. Surely the risk was sufficient for the Supreme Court to ask itself, 'If some legislature fails to act, what happens next?'

What *would* happen next? It is no answer to say, 'Shut down the schools and the legislature will do its duty.' But are federal courts all over the country to decide the policy questions, levy the taxes, and distribute the revenues? Not to act would be to acknowledge judicial futility. To act would be to adopt a tax and fiscal policy for the State. It might even become necessary to set up the machinery to make the policy effective. In addition to questions of competency, those of legitimacy would surely arise. Even in the case of legislative default, does a federal court—usually a single judge—have legitimate power to levy taxes on a people without their consent, and to decide where and how public money shall be spent? Nor would this be the end of the road. There is obvious risk of a collision arising between the court and the political authorities at some subsequent date if the court is forced to act and the legislature thereafter chooses a different programme.

Although other courts acted more vigorously,[1] it is easy to sympathize with the Supreme Court's hesitancy to rush into this kind of morass in the litigation over school finance. Prudence may have been the better part of wisdom in declining so vast and speculative a new undertaking at a time when school desegregation already strains judicial resources. But on at least some other fronts lower courts are pushing ahead with the imposition of affirmative constitutional obligations despite all the difficulties entailed. Consider one last example.

Bryce Hospital is part of mental health facilities of the State of Alabama. A class suit was brought in a federal court on behalf of the guardians of all the patients confined at Bryce Hospital for the purpose of compelling reconstruction of the physical facilities and the improvement of the health services on the theory that the existing conditions violated the patients' constitutional rights. The federal district court sustained the claim:

They unquestionably have a constitutional right to receive such individual treatment as will give each of them a realistic opportunity to be cured or to improve his or her mental condition. . . . The failure to provide suitable and adequate treatment for the mentally ill cannot be justified by lack of staff or facilities.[2]

---

[1] e.g. *Serrano* v. *Priest*, 5 Cal. 3d 584, 487 P.2d 1241 (1971); *Robinson* v. *Cahill*, 62 N.J. 473, 303 A.2d 273 (1973).

[2] *Wyatt* v. *Stickney*, 344 F. Supp. 373, 374 (M.D. Ala. 1972). Analogous cases are collected in *Donaldson* v. *O'Connor*, 493 F. Supp. 507 (5th Cir. 1974), affirmed upon narrower grounds, 43 U.S. Law Wk. 4929 (1975).

Later, after hearing elaborate expert testimony the judge entered a long and detailed order requiring elaborate physical alterations of the facility and new methods of custodial and medical care. For example, in prescribing physical renovation the decree goes into such detail as: 'Thermostatically controlled hot water shall be provided in adequate quantities and maintained at the required temperature for patient or residential use (110° F at the fixture) and for mechanical dishwashing and laundry use (180° F at the equipment).'[1]

With respect to medical and other personnel, the judge laid out the exact number to be employed in each job classification per 250 patients. With respect to medical treatment the judge prescribed how plans for individualized treatment should be developed and what medical records should be kept.

The federal court was fully aware that it was ordering the Alabama Legislature to meet in special session and vote large appropriations.

In the event, though, that the Legislature fails to satisfy its well-defined constitutional obligation, and the Mental Health Board, because of lack of funding or any other legally insufficient reason, fails to implement fully the standards herein ordered, it will be necessary for the Court to take affirmative steps, including appointing a master, to ensure that proper funding is realized. . . .[2]

Thus, an individual federal judge became, in effect, the chief executive or administrator of Bryce Hospital. He also superseded the judgment of the Alabama Legislature in appropriating funds and, indirectly, in issuing bonds or levying taxes. The law reports do not show how far the decrees were obeyed.

Despite the difficulties the Bryce Hospital case may well prove a more reliable harbinger than the decision on school finance. Broadly speaking, the accepted domestic

[1] 344 F. Supp. at 382.   [2] Id. at 394.

philosophy of the eighteenth and nineteenth centuries in the United States laid upon government chiefly the duty of preventing extreme forms of aggression by one man against another, and beyond that to leave men alone to work out their own spiritual and economic salvation. In the 1930s political philosophy came to accept in theory as well as practice the principle that government is not merely a policeman but has affirmative obligations to meet the basic needs of citizens: for subsistence, shelter, jobs, education and—more recently—medical care. Somehow constitutional law must cope with the change. As the dependence of the citizen upon government activities increases, so will grow the proportion of cases in which the critical issues of human liberty, equality, and dignity depend upon how well the government is satisfying its obligations, rather than upon whether the government should leave the individual to himself. The Court will scarcely perform its historical function of protecting the individual in his relation with the State unless substantive constitutional rights and the processes of constitutional adjudication can be adapted so as to retain vitality despite the difficulties of the new milieu. This is the next great challenge of American constitutionalism.

V

CONSTITUTIONALISM AND
POLITICIZATION

THAT the Supreme Court plays a partly political role—
that it makes public policy under the doctrine of judicial
review—is all too obvious. That it is partly bound by law
is equally obvious to anyone who understands the self-
discipline of the legal method. The hard question is one
of degree: how large or small a political role should the
Court play?

This general question has two parts: (1) How far
should the Court confine constitutional adjudication to
cases and remedies traditionally fit for judicial determination; contrariwise, how far should it expand judicial
intervention into the affairs of other branches of government? (2) To what extent should the Justices' decisions
and orders be guided by the considerations of policy that
would control them if they were Platonic Guardians, and
to what extent by law—by criteria and standards that a
judge may deem binding even though he would reach
the opposite conclusion if he were free? Implicit in the
second question are the subordinate inquiries I have
mentioned from time to time concerning the extent of
the Court's duty to defer to legislative and executive
determinations.[1]

[1] See p. 14 and pp. 33–6 above.

The Constitution gives no answers to these questions, nor even a verbal standard to which they can be referred. The Court's answers have varied from time to time, and individual Justices have debated the questions with their contemporaries. The questions are pressing today because the Chief Justiceship of Earl Warren brought a period of extraordinary creativity in constitutional law which has greatly enlarged the role of the Supreme Court in American government and further politicized the process of constitutional adjudication. I have tried to illustrate the principal changes in previous lectures but they are worth summarizing before going on to inquire into their implications.

The most striking aspect of constitutional adjudication under the Warren Court was its vigorous use as an instrument of reform. The decisions discussed in my second lecture enlarged the freedom of the press to investigate and publish charges against public figures by sweeping away 175 years of settled law. The school desegregation cases overturned not only the constitutional precedents built up over three-quarters of a century but the social structure of an entire region. When the Court held that the apportionment of seats in legislative bodies must achieve approximate *per capita* representation, it was invalidating long-settled political arrangements and declaring that the composition of the legislatures of all but one or two of the fifty States was unconstitutional. It would be easy to multiply examples.

Some of the changes, but not all, result from reading into the generalities of the Due Process and Equal Protection Clauses notions of wise and fundamental policy which are not even faintly suggested by the words of the Constitution, and which lack substantial support in other conventional sources of law. The abortion decisions of the Burger Court and the reapportionment cases decided by its predecessor are dramatic examples. In numerous areas the Justices have rejected other precepts of judicial deference to the legislative process by making their own findings upon underlying questions of fact and by appraising and balancing opposing interests.

As explained in the fourth lecture, the Court has embarked upon the imposition of large-scale affirmative obligations, some as remedies for past violations of the Constitution but others as interpretations of what the Constitution itself requires.

The frequency with which the Court decides constitutional issues, the extent of its interference with the Legislative and Executive Branches, and the potential for collision have all been increased by a series of procedural changes which are too technical for discussion here but whose cumulative effect is to move away from the view that constitutional adjudication is only collateral to the essential judicial task of deciding lawsuits and towards the notion that the primary function of the Supreme Court of the United States is to ensure that other organs of government observe constitutional limitations.[1]

Although these trends continue in many lower courts, it is proper to add that in the Supreme Court, where there are now four Nixon appointees including Chief Justice Burger, the pace of change has slowed and in some instances, perhaps, the trend has been reversed. The Burger Court does not respond to humanitarian, libertarian, and egalitarian values with all the enthusiasm of its predecessor. It is more worried by complexities, crosscurrents, and needs for accommodation that refuse to yield to optimistic generalizations. A court more con-

[1] The principal changes have been the relaxation of the requirements of standing (*Flast* v. *Cohen*, 392 U.S. 83, 1968); the expansion of the declaratory judgment (*Katzenback* v. *McClung*, 379 U.S. 294, 1964), the use of the class action (*Roe* v. *Wade*, 410 U.S. 113, 1973), and the narrowing of the category of non-justiciable political questions (*Baker* v. *Carr*, 369 U.S. 186, 1962; *Powell* v. *McCormack*, 395 U.S. 486, 1969).

cerned with the preservation of old substantive values than the articulation of a new spirit is likely to find fewer occasions for rendering activist decisions even though the Justices are not restrained by a modest conception of the judicial function. There are strong indications, however, that the new Justices will not revert to the philosophy of judicial self-restraint when an existing rule offends their policy preferences. The judgment in the abortion cases held statutes prohibiting or regulating abortion in at least forty States to be unconstitutional, sweeping away established law supported by both recent votes as well as moral themes dominant in American life for more than a century, in favour of what seven Justices took to be the wiser view of an actively debated question. There are similar signs in decisions in the area loosely denominated 'women's rights'. The success which losers in the political process enjoyed in using constitutional litigation as an instrument of creative social policy under the Warren Court keeps the pressure alive.

Has the Judicial Branch over-expanded its role in American government and over-politicized the process of constitutional adjudication? Nearly all the rules of constitutional law written by the Warren Court relative to individual and political liberty, equality, and criminal justice, impress me as wiser and fairer than the rules they replace. I would support nearly all as important reforms if proposed in a legislative chamber or a constitutional convention. In appraising them as judicial rulings, however, I find it necessary to ask whether an excessive price was paid by enlarging the sphere and changing the nature of constitutional adjudication. The changes made in governmental institutions today may affect the results tomorrow by reducing the effectiveness of the institutions and the justice of their determinations. One can evade the challenge with Keynes's quip, 'In the long run we shall all be dead', but there remains the duty resulting from our common humanity with future generations.

Two institutional worries result from recent activism in constitutional adjudication. First, there is concern that the Court may sacrifice the power of legitimacy that attaches to decisions within the traditional judicial sphere rendered on the basis of conventional legal criteria, and so may disable itself from performing the narrower but none the less vital constitutional role that all assign to it. Second, there is fear that excessive reliance upon courts instead of self-government through democratic processes may deaden a people's sense of moral and political responsibility for their own future, especially in matters of liberty, and may stunt the growth of political capacity that results from the exercise of the ultimate power of decision.

I

The most important quality of law in a free society is the power to command acceptance and support from the community so as to render force unnecessary, or necessary only upon a small scale against a few recalcitrants. I call this quality the 'power of legitimacy' because it appears to attach to those commands of established organs of government which are seen to result from their performance in an authorized fashion of the functions assigned to them. Such commands, and only such, are legitimate.

The Judicial Branch is uniquely dependent upon the power of legitimacy when engaged in constitutional adjudication; and belief in the legitimacy of its constitutional decisions is therefore a matter of prime importance. The rulings thwart powerful interests. The issues arouse the deepest political emotions. Although the courts control neither the purse nor the sword, their decrees often run against the Executive, set aside the will of the Congress, and dictate to a State. Compliance results from the belief that in such cases the courts are legitimately performing the function assigned to them, and that it is important that the function be preserved. It was the power of legitimacy that produced the public outcry which in turn compelled obedience when President Nixon announced his intention to disregard Judge Sirica's order to produce the Watergate Tapes despite its affirmation by the Court of Appeals. It is to the same power that we must look to induce other branches of government to give support when necessary even to constitutional decisions of which they disapprove.

Without the power of legitimacy, moreover, the Judicial Branch would be exceedingly vulnerable to assaults and reprisals from other branches of government. In *Marbury* v. *Madison*[1] the Secretary of State, following the directions of President Jefferson, ignored the process served upon him. Shortly before, Congress changed the dates of the Supreme Court's terms in order to prevent a timely ruling upon a constitutional question. After the Civil War the Court was deprived of a portion of its appellate jurisdiction in order to prevent its ruling upon the actions of military authority.[2] In the 1950s bills gathered congressional support, although they never became law, looking to sharp curtailment of the Court's jurisdiction in areas in which it had recently rendered unpopular decisions.[3] President Nixon's anti-busing legislation was another direct attack upon the Court's authority which was barely defeated. President Franklin Roosevelt unsuccessfully sought legislation enabling him to pack the Court with new Justices committed to his constitutional philosophy.

The power of the Supreme Court to command acceptance and support not only for its decisions but also for its role in government seems to depend upon a sufficiently

[1] 5 U.S. (1 Cranch) 137 (1803).
[2] *Ex parte* McCardle, 74 U.S. (8 Wall.) 506 (1868).
[3] The political battle is recounted in Murphy, *Congress and the Court* (1962).

widespread conviction that it is acting legitimately, that is, performing the functions assigned to it, and only those functions, in the manner assigned. The conviction of which I speak is the resultant of many voices, not all carrying equal weight: of the opinion of the legal profession, of attitudes in the Executive and in Congress, of the response in State governments, of the press, and of public opinion. But since judicial supremacy upon constitutional questions is a product of institutional development rather than deliberate mandate, the Framers provided no charter by which to measure the legitimate scope and nature of constitutional adjudication. Anyone seeking to determine what role the Supreme Court may play legitimately is driven to examine the sources of acceptance and support in the Nation, upon which reliance must be ultimately placed to give legitimacy to constitutional rulings thwarting other branches of government and even the expressed wish of a majority of the people.

Surely history is the chief source of legitimacy for the basic idea of constitutional adjudication. The Court has long had to decide some constitutional questions, chiefly those arising out of our federalism, for reasons given in the first lecture; and its performance has proved acceptable. Whether it is because of 'the dull traditional habit of mankind' or for some other reason, 'yesterday's institutions are', as Bagehot said, 'accepted as the best for today', all other things being equal, 'and the most easy to get obeyed because they inherit the reverence which others must win'.[1] To this we may link the general acceptance of the courts as forums for resolving a wide variety of judicially cognizable cases and controversies—a role to which constitutional adjudication is readily acceptable as an appendage, provided that we do not make the mistake of severing the two, or of making the tail so big that it wags the dog. But history will not make a

[1] Bagehot, *The English Constitution* (Fontana ed., 1963), pp. 64-5.

new role legitimate in the eyes of the judge, nor a radically and observably new role legitimate in the eyes of the people. Here the 'dull traditional habit of mankind' may aid those who challenge decisions as usurpations.

There is a school of political scientists in the United States that likens the Court to purely political agencies. The Court should do whatever it can—they say—to carry out the policies it deems desirable. Like other politicians the Court should consciously build a coalition of interest-groups, dependent upon judicial aid because they are under-represented elsewhere in government but strong enough collectively to sustain the Court against attacks. As the Court is a clientele agency, we should expect it to follow the pattern of other clientele agencies in acting to create and reinforce its own supporting interests. Part of the clientele is said to be the bench and bar, another part the 'interest-groups' naïve enough to keep on believing the 'judicial myth' that judges are influenced by law and sincerely seek unbiased decisions referrable as often as possible to general and more or less objective standards. 'If the myth of the Court is destroyed in the law schools, the Court loses power', it is said; '. . . the real problem is how the Supreme Court can pursue its policy goals without violating those popular and professional expectations of neutrality, which are an important factor in our legal tradition and a principal source of the Court's prestige.'[1]

Although it may fit the jargon of sociology to describe as an interest-group those who share a common belief in the integrity of the judicial process, surely there is for the judge himself as well as for the people a vast difference between, on the one hand, pursuing the goals of impartial justice *under law* to the satisfaction of those who share this aspiration and, on the other hand, arranging airline routes, highway subsidies, and television allotments to the

[1] Shapiro, *Law and Politics in the Supreme Court* (1964), p. 31.

satisfaction of those who enjoy the benefits. Nor is it possible to keep the 'myth of the Court' alive without living by it enough of the time to give it some reality. Law professors cannot keep a myth alive if political scientists are able to expose the fiction because of their greater candour or truer perception.

But the real vice in substituting a manipulative for a moral view of the judge's role lies much deeper. At the core of the Court's strength is impartiality and independence, and the Justices' freedom from every form of commitment or self-interest. I am not speaking only of freedom from the crasser forms of obligation and ambition, but of a cast of mind free so far as humanly possible from the ties of personal and group loyalties and implied commitments. Nothing can hurt the Court more than for a Justice to continue to maintain political or professional ties with members of the Executive or Legislative Branch or with private organizations. To seek to serve the interests of a clientele—the liberal press, the black, the poor, the extreme political groups, the American Civil Liberties Union, the Office of Economic Opportunity lawyers—is not the same as to seek to find and serve our society's long-range fundamental values appropriately expressed in constitutional law. Serving a clientele implies a degree of commitment apart from merit. Clientele interests and long-range societal values do not *always* overlap. Nor does one get near to describing a Holmes, a Brandeis, a Black, a Warren, or a Harlan by saying that he served a clientele of group-interests that reinforced the Court's position.

Similarly, although the general outlook of an appointee may often be predictable enough and would be taken into account by any President, 'value-packing' the Court in the sense of appointing men so committed to one set of values that all would vote together on a variety of issues in predictable ways would soon raise questions of legitimacy, and thus undermine both the Court and the impact of its decisions. One of the chief dangers of excessive politicization is its tendency to feed upon itself. If constitutional decisions lose their roots in law, such pressures as there are to appoint Justices steeped in the legal tradition would diminish, the decisions would become more political, and the descending spiral accelerate.

A few years ago, seeking to develop in the class-room the possible differences between the function of Congress in deciding whether to enact a measure and the function of the Court in ruling upon its constitutionality once enacted, I put to a student a hypothetical bill forbidding strikes for higher wages in the construction industry, and then developed to the best of my ability all the considerations pro and con that would be taken into account by a detached, conscientious, and wise legislator, uninfluenced by personal ambition, party loyalty, or other commitment. I then asked the student what, if this was the function of the legislator, was the function of the Court. Was it to act as a supra-legislature, going over the same ground? If not, how should the definition of the judicial function be limited? The student replied that my question was based upon a false hypothesis because no legislature acted or was even expected to act in the manner I had described; what I had described, he insisted, was the process of decision to be followed by the Court. While I reject the student's description of the judicial function in constitutional adjudication, he struck near a different truth. The political branches are the forums where group-interests are served, coalitions are built, loyalties are formed, and obligations respected. The function of the Court—the role implicitly assigned to it by history as well as the fact of its having been created as a court—is illuminated by contrast with the political branches. Its decisions are legitimate only when it seeks to dissociate itself from individual or group interests, and to judge by disinterested and more objective standards.

The ability to rationalize a constitutional judgment honestly in terms of principles referrable to legal precedent and other accepted sources of law is, by the lawyers' tradition, an essential major ingredient of the Court's power to command acceptance and support. In the case of judicial rulings the power of legitimacy is thought to depend largely upon the realization that the major influence in a decision is not personal fiat, but principles which bind the judges as well as the litigants, and which apply uniformly to all men not only today but yesterday and tomorrow.

The use of constitutional adjudication as an instrument of reform intensifies the difficulty of explaining constitutional decisions by reference to accepted sources of law. A nay-saying court engaged in invalidating novel legislation upon constitutional grounds has little need to overrule previous decisions. A reforming court is constantly overturning settled precedents. The costs are illustrated by *Brown* v. *Board of Education*.[1] The failure to follow *Plessy* v. *Ferguson*[2] and other cases upholding racial segregation in equal facilities damaged the principle of legitimacy because men disappointed by the new decision were able to excuse disobedience by saying, 'The desegregation ruling is not law, but the dictate of nine men. In time, with nine different men, the Court will return to its earlier decisions.' The strain thus put upon the Court's position, in terms of the capacity to do one of the major jobs assigned to law, did not pass unobserved in subsequent litigation.

I am far from suggesting that the decision in the school desegregation cases was wrong even in the most technical sense. To have adhered to the doctrine of 'separate but equal' would have ignored not only the revolution sweep-

[1] 347 U.S. 483 (1954).   [2] 163 U.S. 537 (1896).

ing the world, but the moral sense of civilization. Law must be binding even upon the highest court, but it must also meet the needs of men and match their ethical sensibilities. The dilemma lies at the root of Anglo-American jurisprudence. There have always been occasions when the courts, to shape the law to these objectives, have had to pay the price of revealing that judges sometimes make law to suit the occasion. Nor should we forget that not to pay that price may even defeat the object of obtaining voluntary compliance, because law, to command consent, must deserve it.

No other Anglo-American court has ever overturned so many precedents and made so much new law in so short a time as the Supreme Court under Chief Justice Warren. Yet the prestige of the Supreme Court is surely greater than that of other branches of government today, and I am inclined to think that it has never been higher. The continuing attachment of the American people to constitutionalism was demonstrated when President Nixon vainly attempted to withhold the Watergate Tapes and other evidence subpoenaed for the Grand Jury. Are we to explain this reaction by some peculiarity in the era of the Warren Court? Or has the legal profession exaggerated the importance of judicial adherence to a rule of law in gaining legitimacy for constitutional decisions?

Perhaps some light can be shed upon the problem by asking whether constitutionalism would be well served by continuing disregard for precedent after a new conservative Justice replaces a libertarian one, thus constituting a pretty firm majority opposed to some of the leading decisions of the Warren Court in the area of criminal law. That the conservative majority would not extend the trend of Warren Court decisions but trim them back is certain; this much is a traditional part of the judicial process. Would the new Court again 'reform' the law by overruling such 'reforming' Warren precedents as the rulings excluding illegally obtained evidence and confessions obtained in violation of the *Miranda* warnings? Conservatives usually stress the legal side of constitutional adjudication and adhere to the law revealed in precedent, but these cases could put their belief in the importance of the idea of law to a severer test. Those who tend to approve unrestrained activism because of the decisions reached by the Warren Court can also use the examples to test their philosophy. Should five Justices who firmly believe the rule excluding illegally obtained evidence to be unwise and destructive of justice use their power to overrule it, just as five predecessors used their power to install it ten years ago? If so, what would be the effect of a succession of reforms and re-reforms upon the position of the Court and the idea of law? If not, how was the position of the Warren Court better when it overruled decades of precedent?

In my view a clear-cut line of precedents, not shown to be logically inconsistent with a wider body of constitutional decisions, should be given great weight in later cases. I cannot measure the weight, but it should be so great—I think—as to outweigh the arguments for change unless one is pretty clear that the change is impelled by one of the deeper lasting currents of human thought that give direction to the law. Such major reversals of precedent as the reapportionment and school desegregation decisions fall into the latter category. So do some, but not all, of the constitutional changes in criminal procedure.[1]

It is at this point that the legitimating influence of the

---

[1] e.g. *Gideon* v. *Wainwright*, 372 U.S. 335 (1963), which overruled *Betts* v. *Brady*, 316 U.S. 455 (1942), and held that due process requires the State to supply counsel to the indigent accused in all serious criminal cases, is plainly correct. I have much more doubt about *Mapp* v. *Ohio*, 367 U.S. 643 (1961), overruling *Wolf* v. *Colorado*, 338 U.S. 25 (1949), and a long line of decisions, even though I would favour the exclusion of illegally obtained evidence as an original question. In the latter instance there are strong arguments for either

idea of natural law becomes important. We should use different words today: 'impersonal and durable principles', 'enduring values', 'fundamental aspirations', 'vital lessons of liberty and equal opportunity', 'human rights', and so on; but the very persistence of such evocative, rather than sharply definitive, phrases attests the strength of our natural law inheritance *as authority for legal change.* 'What drives us back from time to time to search further, to question outright what are our purposes,' Lord Radcliffe observes, 'is the insistence of the layman, the man who is not versed in law, that it shall stand for something more, for some vindication of a sense of right and wrong that is not merely provisional nor just the product of a historical process.'[1] Natural law in this sense legitimizes change, if indeed it does not impel it; and it legitimates for the public and perhaps even for the judge himself a measure of constitutional adjudication as an instrument of reform.

Of course, natural law provides no definition of the substantive scope of the judge's commission. Some Supreme Court Justices and commentators have found the entire notion so vague an invitation to decision by personal fiat as to reject reliance upon substantive due process. Here we come back to the questions left open at the end of my second lecture.[2] What are we to say of the Supreme Court's decision holding that the Due Process Clause forbids a State to interfere with a woman's right to an abortion? What of the judicial method?

My colleague John Ely criticizes the abortion decision on the ground that there is nothing in the Constitution that marks freedom to have an abortion as something special: 'A neutral and durable principle may be a

---

view and, as I see the situation, any candid judge would have to acknowledge that unless he follows precedent, he is simply expressing a personal preference.

[1] *The Law and its Compass,* (1970), p. 78.   [2] See p. 55 above.

thing of beauty and a joy forever. But if it lacks connection with any value the Constitution marks as special it is not a constitutional principle and the Court has no business imposing it.'[1]

My own view is less rigid. I find sufficient connection in the Due Process Clause. All agree that the clause calls for some measure of judicial review of legislative enactments, and from that point forward all must be done by judicial construct with no real guidance from the document. Nothing in the document dictates reading the federal Bill of Rights into the Fourteenth Amendment as either a source or a limitation of fundamental values, nor does the document suggest restrained review in some cases and strict review in others. The Court's persistent resort to notions of substantive due process for almost a century attests the strength of our natural law inheritance in constitutional adjudication, and I think it unwise as well as hopeless to resist it.

My criticism of *Roe* v. *Wade* is that the Court failed to establish the legitimacy of the decision by articulating a precept of sufficient abstractness to lift the ruling above the level of a political judgment based upon the evidence currently available from the medical, physical, and social sciences. Nor can I articulate such a principle— unless it be that a State cannot interfere with individual decisions relating to sex, procreation, and family with only a moral or philosophical State justification: a principle which I cannot accept or believe will be accepted by the American people.[2] The failure to confront the issue in principled terms leaves the opinion to read like a set of hospital rules and regulations, whose validity is good enough this week but will be destroyed with new statistics upon the medical risks of childbirth and abortion or new

[1] Ely, 'The Wages of Crying Wolf', 82 Yale L.J. 920, 949 (1973).

[2] The rulings bringing patently offensive utterances within the First Amendment suggest that the notion may influence some Justices. See pp. 45–8 above.

advances in providing for the separate existence of a foetus. Neither historian, layman, nor lawyer will be persuaded that all the details prescribed in *Roe* v. *Wade* are part of either natural law or the Constitution. Constitutional rights ought not to be created under the Due Process Clause unless they can be stated in principles sufficiently absolute to give them roots throughout the community and continuity over significant periods of time, and to lift them above the level of the pragmatic political judgments of a particular time and place.

A different example may help to clarify my meaning. Suppose that in 1984 the question were to arise whether a State would violate the Fourteenth Amendment by permanently implanting an electrode in the minds of individuals with turbulent, aggressive, and destructive personalities, without their consent, in order to calm their aggressions without *substantially* interfering with their capacity for usefulness or their enjoyment of existence. A conventional legal method of resolving this kind of issue, which appears to have been followed in the abortion cases, is to master all the data provided by physiologists, neurologists, psychologists, and social scientists, and then to determine whether the gain to society outweighs any harm to the individuals affected. For the Court to invalidate this hypothetical State law under the Due Process Clause upon such a calculus would, in my view, abuse the judicial function. I would think it quite proper to hold that the Due Process Clause's guarantee of liberty forbids a State to tamper with the human mind or spirit without consent—not 'under some circumstances', nor 'without compelling justification', but 'absolutely'. The point I seek to emphasize is the contrast between a judgmental balance of shifting evidence or values and a declaration of virtually absolute and enduring principle.

I suspect that support for increasing the role of the

judiciary also flows from the basic philosphy of the separation of powers, which looks not merely to opposing one centre of power to another, but to increasing the places to which a citizen may turn for relief of his grievance. Lord Acton remarked of federalism: 'By multiplying centres of government and discussion it promotes the diffusion of political knowledge and the maintenance of healthy and independent opinion.'[1] The observation seems equally applicable to the separation of powers. Given the size and concerns of the political and bureaucratic arms of government, the judiciary is increasingly often the only place where relief can be obtained. Without constitutional adjudication not sanctioned by the strict judicial method, we should still be tolerating a caste system and suffering the inequity of legislative malapportionment. The press would be constrained by fear of suits for libel or prosecutions for contempt of court in publishing discreditable news of public figures; and in some States poor persons charged with crime would still be forced to trial without the assistance of counsel. These are not matters to which Congress or State legislatures would attend. Lord Justice Scarman's Hamlyn Lectures show that doubts are also rising whether in Britain freedom of speech, the rights of the accused, and other civil liberties can safely be left to the Parliament without provision for a stronger, more creative judicial role.

II

I turn at the end to two chief sources of doubt about the wisdom of assigning the Supreme Court a larger and more political role in government even if it has power to sustain it. One objection was most eloquently stated by Judge Learned Hand:

[1] Acton, 'The History of Freedom in Antiquity', reprinted in *Essays on Freedom and Power* (Himmelfarb ed.), p. 72.

For myself it would be most irksome to be ruled by a bevy of Platonic Guardians, even if I knew how to choose them, which I assuredly do not. If they were in charge, I should miss the stimulus of living in a society where I have, at least theoretically, some part in the direction of public affairs. Of course, I know how illusory would be the belief that my vote determined anything; but nevertheless when I go to the polls I have a satisfaction in the sense that we are all engaged in a common venture.[1]

I should be no less irked than Judge Hand if the Supreme Court were to void an ordinance adopted in the open Town Meeting in the New England town in which I live—a meeting in which all citizens can participate— but I should have little such feeling about a statute enacted by the Massachusetts legislature in the normal political pattern, and none about a law made in that normal pattern by the Congress of the United States. Perhaps my sense of the matter is distorted by years of advocacy in constitutional cases, but it appears to me that modern government is simply too large and too remote, and too few issues are fought out in elections, for a citizen to feel much more sense of participation in the legislative process than the judicial. Nor does the Supreme Court's intervention lessen my sense that we are all engaged in a common adventure.

Professor James Bradley Thayer, Judge Hand's teacher of constitutional law, emphasized another aspect of the same objection:

It should be remembered that the exercise of [the power of judicial review], even when unavoidable, is always attended with a serious evil, namely that the correction of legislative mistakes comes from the outside, and the people thus lose the political experience, and the moral education and stimulus that comes from fighting the question out in the ordinary way, and correcting their own errors. The tendency of a common and easy resort to this great function . . .

[1] Hand, *The Bill of Rights* (Atheneum, 1959), pp. 73–4.

is to dwarf the political capacity of the people, and to deaden its sense of moral responsibility.[1]

Was Thayer right? Or does the Court at its best assist in the process of education? The great opinions of the Court seem to me to help to make us what we are by telling us what we may be. The 'one man, one vote' cases revived majoritarian democracy. *Brown* v. *Board of Education* upset habits so ingrained that their viciousness could be conveniently ignored so long as the Court was silent. Other decisions expanded political liberty and brought more nearly equal justice into the criminal courts. These changes would have been long delayed—perhaps they would not have happened—if the country had waited for legislative action. Still, one cannot accurately say either that the Court forced the decisions upon an unwilling majority or that the decisions deadened the sense of moral responsibility or dwarfed the political capacity of the people. The Reapportionment Cases evoked widespread popular support. The resistance to the desegregation cases is still widespread and genuine, but there is no doubt that most of the American people reject apartheid when forced to face up to the question, and the constitutional decision stirred up a wealth of supportive political action which has immeasurably improved the opportunities of former victims of discrimination.

Constitutional adjudication depends, I think, upon a delicate, symbiotic relation. The Court must know us better than we know ourselves. Its opinions may, as I have said, sometimes be the voice of the spirit, reminding us of our better selves. In such cases the Court has an influence just the reverse of what Thayer feared; it provides a stimulus and quickens moral education. But while the opinions of the Court can help to shape our national understanding of ourselves, the roots of its decisions must be already in the nation. The

[1] Thayer, *John Marshall* (1920), pp. 106–7.

aspirations voiced by the Court must be those the community is willing not only to avow but in the end to live by. The legitimacy of the great constitutional decisions rests upon the accuracy of the Court's perception of this kind of common will and upon the Court's ability, by expressing its perception, ultimately to command a consensus.

When asked to explain the source of our constitutionalism, John Lord O'Brian, a great American lawyer, replied by quoting Alfred North Whitehead's observation that no other people in the history of mankind had ever shown such innate qualities of tolerance and co-operation. Tolerance and the will to co-operate flow from belief in the worthwhileness of the common human enterprise—despite its faults, despite our selfishness, and even though we can perceive its goals only dimly. For me, belief in the value of the enterprise is an article of faith. Whether Whitehead was really right—whether enough of us still have enough belief in the worthwhileness of our common fate for the spirit of tolerance and the will to co-operate to survive in sufficient measure—I must leave to those whose powers of observation are uncommitted.